GOD IS BUSY FIXING THINGS

BY PASTOR JIM WALTER

Xulon
PRESS

God Is Busy Fixing Things
by Pastor Jim Walter

Printed in the United States of America

ISBN 9781615799237

Unless otherwise indicated, Bible quotations are taken from the King James Version of the Bible.

www.xulonpress.com

Acknowledgements

There are several people to which I wish to express my gratitude for their help in getting this book published. First, I wish to thank Jim Dodge for his many, many hours of typing and making corrections from my handwritten manuscript. Secondly, my wife and daughter also did much typing and correcting more of my grammar and spelling. Then, to all those who encouraged me to write this book and to all those who have read separate chapters from the book and given suggestions to make the book more readable, I just say, "Thank you."

Dedication

"Therefore let no man glory in men. For all things are yours: Whether Paul or Apollos or Cephas, or the world, or life, or death, or things present, or things to come, all are yours; and you are Christ's and Christ is Gods." I Cor. 3:21-23

To all those co-laborers together with Christ that could be added to Paul, Apollos and Cephas over the past two thousand years who have left their writings behind for me to read and study I dedicate this book. They are mine. They have been my pastors and mentors who taught, reproved, corrected and instructed me to walk in love and righteous paths. Most of all they encouraged me and helped me increase in the knowledge of God and grow in grace and knowledge of Jesus Christ. They were many, most wrote over the past five hundred years or so since the invention of the printing press.

To list all their names here would take more space than we have in this short dedication. There was Martin Luther, John Calvin, John Bunyan, Adoniram Judson, Hudson Taylor, Andrew Murray, F.B.Meyer, Charles Spurgeon,. Campbell Morgan and A.W.Tozer, to name a few. They were men Christ gave to His Church.

The effects God made in lives through their preaching, teaching, and obeying His Word continues on through their writings.

An illustration of this just came over my computer as I was listing the names above. An E-Mail from missionary friends in Thailand (Formerly Burma) spoke of Adoniram Judson and his writings he left behind more than one hundred fifty years ago when he was the

Pioneer Christian missionary there in Burma. They are still being read and used there today. As I read that E-mail my mind went back more than fifty years to a time of great stress in the ministry I was then experiencing. It was reading The Memoirs of Adoniram Judson along with the encouragement from several pastor friends that God used to keep me faithful to the work to which He had called me.

To that long list of Gods fellow laborers and their books I dedicate this book and add it to that number with the prayer that as God used their writings in my life, He might use this book to affect other lives for His Glory.

Preface

This book is different. It is all about Gods work. It's not about God blessing the work we do for Him. It's about being one with Him in that which He is doing. It's about THE HOME and THE CHURCH. (The two God ordained Institutions) It's about the transformation of individual lives, people like you and me. That's Gods work. We can't do it, but we can be co-laborers with Him as was Paul and Apollos in I Cor. 3.

Before you start reading let me forewarn you, everything you read is not going to be pretty. That old deceiver, divider, and destroyer (Gods archenemy, the devil) that invaded His crowning creation (the family) in Genesis 3 and 4 is just as active today as he was back there in the first family.

Added to the fact that Satan is just as active as ever, totally bent on disgracing Gods Holy name, there is that old sin principle that is in everyone of us (called the flesh or the old man) ever ready to express itself in all sorts of selfish sinful actions and attitudes.

Finally as a band of Pilgrims whose citizenship is in heaven, living in a world and culture that is continually becoming more ungodly, exerting its influence to force us into its mold (as it did Lot of old), there are ever more and more of the prince of this worlds snares to trap us on every hand.

This book is about Gods work, the work He is doing twenty four hours each day seven days a week, not merely what He does for several hours on Sunday while His people are gathered together. Come along with me and see what takes place in the lives of those in whom God is working. Actually what we are going to see is the outward circumstances and results surrounding and flowing from lives in whom God is working. Believe me there is never a dull moment in the life of a co-laborer with God. God's archenemy will see to that.

Wouldn't it be great if all of us who claim to have been saved by grace through faith in Jesus Christ could mature to the place where we, in love and obedience to Him, would walk in the good works He has ordained for all his children. Before beginning to read this book please read *Eph.2:8-10, Phil. 2:12-16 and Titus 2:11-15.*

TABLE OF CONTENTS

WHO IS HE?

1. "He is." He is the "*I AM.*" Only He IS. Everything and everyone else "became." He is Eternal, without beginning or end.

2. "He is as He is." His name is "*I AM that I AM.*" Only He is as He is "*the same yesterday, today and forever.*" He is unchangeable.

3. He is as He says He is. He has verbally revealed Himself in His Book that we might know Him, the Eternal unchangeable One.

4. He did what He says He did. He says He spoke the heavens, earth and everything they contain into existence. He made man (mankind) in His Image. When Satan introduced sin into His creation (including mankind) He cursed His whole creation with death. He came to His Own Creation through a supernatural birth, lived a sinless life, died a sinners death, and arose from the dead to redeem His cursed, fallen creation. He ascended back to His Eternal Glory with His Eternal Father with the promise He would return and complete His work of Redemption. Yes He did all He says He did.

5. He is doing what He says He is doing. He says He is ruling over all. He says He is holding all things together (His entire creation) by the Word of His Power. He says He is calling a people out of His cursed, fallen race of mankind to become a family of children like Himself. He says He is changing them from "*glory into*

glory" through His Word by the Power of The Holy Spirit whom He sent to take His place when He ascended back to His Father.

6. He will do what He says He will do. He says He will come again to complete His work of redemption. He says He will fix that which can and, or, will be fixed, take them to be with himself, and cast the remainder out from His presence. He says He will then make New Heavens and New Earth wherein dwells righteousness.

WHO IS HE? HIS NAME IS JEHOVAH (O. T.) JESUS (N.T.)

Who are we?

"What is man that you are mindful of him? Or the son of man, that you visited him?" Hebrews 2:6
In the Image of God we were made long ago
With the purpose divine here His Glory to show.
But we failed Him one day, and like Sheep went astray
Thinking not of the cost, we His likeness had lost.
But from eternity God had in mind,
The work of Calvary, the lost to find.

From His heavens so broad Christ came down earth to trod,
So that men might live again in the Image of God.

Now that I have believed and the Saviour received,
Now that I from the cry of my guilt am relieved,
I will live for my Lord, not for gain or reward,
But for love-thinking of what His grace has restored.

I'll never comprehend Redemption's plan
How Christ could condescend to die for man.
Such a Saviour I'll praise to the end of my days,
As I upward, onward trod in the Image of God.
John Peterson

MARTIN — A MIRACLE
by Pastor Jim Walter

Martin Johnson
Boy that Mother and Dad took in for 10 months.
Windham Summit 1956

"Let me give you my name and address." "Don't bother, just take them and give them a good home."

Those were not the words from one giving a litter of pups away. They were the words of a man giving the last two of his children to us, a young couple he had never seen nor heard of before that day. That was more than fifty two years ago. We took those two children and never saw or even heard from that father again. "Un-believable" you say, and yet; True. Let's go back a little farther and give some background to that which led up to that incident and another incident that took place nearly fifty years later.

My wife and I had been married nearly five years, the last three in a little country pastorate. We had no children and were told it was unlikely we ever would. The thought of adoption had been mentioned to several people. Nothing serious at the time but we had discussed that thought with several friends. It was one of those friends that dropped by one winter Sunday afternoon. He often did this, but this time we could see he was on a mission and one that required urgency.

His first words were: "Are you still interested in getting a child?" "Well yes, but what is the excitement in your voice all about"? "It's like this, I've just found out about a man who is giving all his children away. He had eleven and there are only two left. One is a girl ten years old, the other a boy five years old. I know a widow who will take the girl and thought you might want the boy, but we must get them right away if we want them. I'm going after the girl tomorrow and if you want the boy you can go along and we can also get him."

My first thought was: "Emory, have you gone crazy? Things like this don't just happen." Although not in so many words I expressed this thought to him, and said I had to have more information before I would ever want to get involved in such a transaction.

He assured us everything was on the "up and up." He said he had just come from a prominent family in the community who had taken a baby from this family a year before and had now taken another just recently. They were the ones that had told him about the last two children who were left. He went on to explain that this last baby they had taken was only several days old when they had gotten her several months before, and that the mother had died during the birth of that child.

It was after this the father felt he could not care for his children alone and that he was giving them away one by one. I did not find out until the next day that the father was an alcoholic in the truest sense of the word. Yes, we did go to pick up Isabel and Martin the next morning. I hope I can do justice in describing the events of that meeting, and as well the remainder of that day.

Martin's home was not more than twenty five or thirty miles from where we lived. Emory picked us up about nine a.m. He was a farmer and said he had hurried as fast as he could to get the morning chores done so we could get to the small town as early as possible. I don't know what words to use to describe our emotions as we drove just a short way off the main street in that small town. It was no more than three blocks down across the tracks and we were in a different world. Most of the houses were shacks. Emory was not sure which was the one for which we were looking. Then we saw a man sitting on the top step of a partially fallen down porch. He turned out to be Martin's father. He said he was Martin J Sr. After introducing ourselves he invited us to come inside. Someone, I presume it was the family who had taken the baby that was born when the mother died, had notified him we would be coming.

With his first words I knew he was drinking too much already in the morning. We would later learn from little Martin that he spent as much time in a bar room as he did in his home.

I was totally unprepared for what I was to see in that old shack. There was only one room divided by dirty curtains and blankets hanging from wires. A stove and a few old chairs and a table were all the furniture I saw. From the one so called bedroom I did get a glimpse of, I could see no bed and no dressers of any kind, just a mattress on the dirty wood floor, with clothes laying everywhere. How two adults and eleven children ever lived in that place I'll never know. Mr. J already had Isabel's and Martin's clothes packed to go. I say packed. Actually he handed us two brown grocery bags full of some of the dirtiest, worn out, beyond that which could be called, clothes. We burned nearly all that was in Martins bag that very afternoon.

It was at the door on the way out that I offered Mr. J my name and address which he refused, with this response, "Don't bother, just take them and give them a good home."

I've told that story dozens of times over the years, and the looks on their faces is always the same, just like yours as you are reading this, a look OF TOTAL UNBELIEF.

Little Martin said nothing the entire way home. In fact he just sat there with a blank stare on his face. I thought afterward, maybe this was his first ride in a car. We doubted if he had ever been out of that little town in all his five years.

We arrived home at noon. Emory left us out with Martin and his brown bag of clothes (rags). Martin looked up for the first time since we left his home an hour before. As he looked all around, and then at us, I could see he was frightened. As we entered our house, looking at the clock on the wall I said; "hey, look its time to eat, I'm hungry aren't you hungry to, Martin?" My wife interrupted with two words. "Not yet!", and then whispered in my ear: "That boy has to have a bath before any thing else." She went straight through the kitchen and into the bathroom. In minutes that bath tub was ready for a brand new experience. Little Martin looked at that tub half full of water and was scared to death. It was obvious he had never seen a bath tub before and probably never had a bath either.

Fifteen minutes later that tub had the dirtiest gray water I had ever seen. We dried Martin off and I headed out to the kitchen to get on some lunch while my wife dressed him. I could hear my wife talking half under her breath. I thought she said, "Honey you're not clean yet," and then I heard water running in the tub again. Martin was about to get a second scrubbing. This time my wife said she was going to use some "elbow grease." I hope you who are reading this understand that expression. I know Martin understood by the time she was through rubbing his whole body with that wash cloth and soap. I said "rubbing" not merely using a little soap and then rinsing it off. And you know that water was gray again. Surprisingly Martin gave no resistance through all this. Not one word. In fact it was the next day before we could get anything out of him. We even wondered if he could talk at all.

It was the next evening at the supper table when he finally put several words together. They were "I don't want that." What he did not want was meat and vegetables. When we asked what he would like, he said: "Coffee bread." After several more days and several more meals, we came to the conclusion he did not even know the names of different vegetables. We were sure his major food really was "Coffee bread." It took weeks before he was able to break his addiction to coffee. Yes, I said ADDICTION.

After going to town and getting some good clothes he began to open up and show some emotions, but one thing we never saw him do in the ten months we had him was cry. In so many ways he was such a lovable child, but those first five years of his life had left him with some real problems. Several of them were of a physical nature which needed medical attention. At that time we were in no financial condition to do anything about those.

If you have read my former book <u>Fifty Years a Country Pastor (Shepherd)</u>, we were in the midst of the time I described with these words: "We got hungry, we got tired, and we got irritable toward one another." We had to move into three different houses during those months Martin was with us. Things were bad financially and at the church.

In the midst of this IT happened and we did not even know IT happened until nearly five months after IT happened. My wife was expecting. Now what are we going to do? With no money, a broken down car, the church several weeks behind in my salary, my wife expecting, a little boy we had come to love with problems, and to top it all off, several people in the church who felt we should not have taken him in the first place. Where was God in all this? We began to wonder.

I'm glad little Martin can't remember all that transpired during those ten months he was with us. I am sure they were a lot better than his first five years, but those ten months and the next two years were definitely the most trying years of our fifty seven years of marriage.

My wife and I were so frustrated. We knew some decisions had to be made. Our major problem was financial. We began to feel that maybe those people in the church that thought we should not have gotten Martin were right. But by now, we were strongly bonded to that little guy. We even talked about taking him back to the place we had gotten him but that thought was soon dismissed. There was no way that would ever happen. My wife for a period of time begged me to leave the pastorate. We both were constantly recalling how well off we were when we were both working just a year or so before. But we both knew when we left those jobs we would never again get that kind of money in any country pastorate. There was a lot of unrest in our home during that period. I have often thought about those times and wondered what was going through poor little Martin's mind.

Forty eight years later I would find out that he remembered little of those times. But wait: I'm getting ahead of myself.

In the midst of our dilemma we met Rev. Manderson, an Evangelist. My wife and I poured out our whole situation to him. He referred us to a man in another state that operated a children's home. We contacted him. He immediately responded telling us of a couple who had been married for years and would never be able to have children of their own. He said he would like to bring them to see us and meet Martin. These were not our thoughts at all. We were not sure we wanted to part with Martin permanently. Our thoughts were maybe this home could take him temporarily until we were better able to care for him and his needs.

After a lengthy telephone conversation we did agree for him to bring this couple to meet with us and Martin. It was two weeks before Christmas. They came and it was evident this couple loved children. They immediately took to Martin. After several hours together the man who brought this couple made this suggestion. "Why don't we have Martin go home with this couple over Christmas. They could give him a good Christmas and bring him back after the New Year.

My wife and I went into the next room to discuss the man's suggestion. We did more crying than discussing, but after 10 or 15 minutes decided to go along with the suggestion. As we packed Martins clothes for his big Holiday, I wondered to myself: "Are we not now doing just what his father did ten months before?"

When I saw the smiles on that couples faces as they walked to their car with Martin between them, I knew there was no way they would want to return him in three weeks. I was right. We got the call from the man from the Children's Home the day after New Years day. His Question: "George and Eleanor just love Martin. They would like to keep him." Total silence "They are also ready to bring him back if you say that is what you want."

Our thoughts at that moment: "O God how did we get into this? How can we make such an important decision? What's best for Martin? What's best for us? Most important for everyone, Lord what do you want us to do? If we say keep him, will we ever see him again? What a decision we are being asked to make: With emotions pulling all directions we responded with almost the same words his father said to us nearly a year before: "Keep him, God bless you, and give him a good home. We will always keep him and the Qualmans in our hearts and prayers".

That was the last time we saw or heard from Martin for forty six years. Then six years ago we received a Christmas card with this letter enclosed.

Dear Pastor Walter and Family

I thought I would drop you a line since I know that you and my parents write to each other each year. There is so much to tell and thank the Lord for that I cannot begin to express. But I do want to thank the Lord for you and for giving me a wonderful Christian Mom and Dad. His hand has really been on my life.

Here is a picture of myself and my lovely wife Dollie. We both love the Lord and are serving in the church.

We wish you a Joyous Christmas and Happy New Year. If you are ever in this area I hope you will look us up.

Lovingly in Christ

Martin and Dollie Qualman

Two years later we did make the two thousand mile trip to Phoenix and spent an evening with Martin, Dollie, and his parents none of which we had seen in forty eight years. What a great evening together. To see Martin that night there in their beautiful home and remembering his origin convinced me God was the One who caused us to make that hard decision all those years before. And when we saw his love for Jesus Christ we knew God had been working in his life down through all those years. Certainly God can and does bring good things out of the most impossible situations. Little Martin is absolute evidence of that fact. He is truly "A MIRACLE OF GODS GRACE."

Martin and Dollie Qualman 2002

Pastor Walter, Martin, Doris Walter 2004

SECTION ONE

GOD THROUGH HIS WORD FIXING THINGS
SELF CENTERED SINNERS
BROKEN HOMES
DIVIDED CHURCHES
SHATTERED RELATIONSHIPS

"Daddy, Mommy, why can't we all go home and live together? Please, please, can't we? Can't we?"

"I wish they would decide which side they are on. Last Sunday they were here with us and now they are over there with them."

The first question was asked by three children begging their mother and father, who had divorced, to get back together so they could be a family again.

The second statement was made by a deacon who was leading a group that had split off from a church. They were holding services just ten miles from the church they had left, and the group to whom this deacon was referring was a heart-broken group of God's children that didn't wish to be separated from either of the split groups. They loved them both.

Just as the three children from the first illustration who longed for a loving, united family, the ones whom the deacon was slandering wanted the same for God's Family (the local church). In both cases, the innocent were caught in the middle, and they were the ones who were suffering.

Actually, there was another whose heart was grieved far more than anyone who was involved in either of the aforementioned situations. That One is God, the God of Revelation (the Bible). He is the One Who ordained the family in *GENESIS 2,* and the Church in *ACTS 1 and 2.*

There was also another who, instead of grieving over these incidents, was insidiously rejoicing at the division and destruction he had inflicted on those involved. He appeared in *GENESIS 3* and has been active ever since, doing his best to deceive, divide, and destroy that which God created for His Glory.

Incidents like these have always been with us and have increased at an alarming rate over the last fifty years. One day soon God will say, "Enough." In the meantime, He is still transforming individual lives, building homes, and above all, building His church. It is in this eternal work that He wants you and me who love Him, to be one with Him. It is blessed work, but it is a battle. As God works in and through His own, the Evil One is there each step of the way to counteract, and many times, to counterfeit what He is doing.

I was not involved in the second incident with that local church, but I did witness those three children crying and pleading with their father and mother to go home together and be a family again. Although that incident took place more than sixty years ago, there are tears in my eyes even now as I recall it. It isn't any wonder to me that in the last book of the Old Testament, God said He *hates divorce. (Mal. 1:14-16)*

I also will never forget the response of my sister (yes, my sister, who was sixteen years older than I) as those three children begged Mommy and Daddy to go home together.

Her answer: "We can't do that."

Their question in return: "Why?"

Her reply was, "It's too late. Mommy and Daddy don't love each other anymore."

The truth is, both Mom and Dad had been unfaithful to their marriage vows, and both were involved in extramarital relationships at that time.

Two of those children with their mother (my sister) were living with us (my mother and father, my brother and myself). The other child was living with his father. One Sunday afternoon we met at a park so those three siblings could spend a few hours playing together. It was at the close of those hours of play when it was time to go to their separate homes that these events took place.

The horrible results of that broken home were repeated in the homes of those three children, and I have certainly seen them repeated dozens of times in the years since, even in the lives and homes of those who profess to believe in Jesus Christ.

Only the Grace and Love of God is glue strong enough to bind either a family or local church together so it is able to manifest the "oneness" of unity and harmony before an unbelieving world.

I can attest to the fact that a co-laborer with God, in this work with God, will spend much of his life in God's Word and on his knees if God is going to transform his life and use him in doing the same in others. If the Word he gives forth *"In Season"* (from the pulpit, in public) and *"Out of Season"* (in homes, one on one, wherever) is not the Word God has used in transforming his life, he cannot expect God to use it to transform families, local churches, or individuals like himself. That is what God is doing today. He is busy fixing things; namely, that which got broke in *GENESIS THREE*.

Written in language everyone can understand, are four family situations about which you are about to read, where God preserved the family unit in spite of, or should I say "through" some awful trying, sinful circumstances. These are just four of many similar attacks of Satan, on the home, that every co-laborer with God will face.

The first example involved one of the three children we just talked about. My involvement began fifteen years after the incident in the park, where my sister said, "Mommy and Daddy don't love each other anymore." This incident, coupled with another one that occurred at the same time, helped change the course of my ministry as a pastor, from that time forward.

Summed up in one sentence, God, through Redemption (with ALL that word entails), is in the business of transforming lives for His eternal Glory, and He wants me (one in whom He is working, doing this very thing) to be a co-laborer with Him in doing the same in others. This includes everything from fixing the "rainforest entrance into the church building" (you will read about that entrance later on) to hours of teaching, reproving, correcting, instructing, and encouraging from the Word of God, "in season and out of season," day after day, and many times, on into the night. Just ask the wife of any faithful pastor. Being a faithful under-shepherd and a co-laborer with God is not a 9 to 5 job.

TRANSFORMED LIVES
"Without me you can do nothing" John 15:5

Ruby Mae

It was 1962, and at the time, we were three years into a small town pastorate. God was greatly blessing this local flock with many changed lives. They were understanding, many for the first time, what a living relationship with the Heavenly Shepherd was all about.

My mother was with us for the summer as my father had gone home to be with the Lord several years before. One evening, at the supper table, she said, "Jimmie, I wish you could have a talk with Ruby Mae."

Ruby Mae was my niece and just seven years younger than I. We had lived in the same home for a number of years during the Second World War, as her father was in the service. Her mother, my older sister, had moved in with us along with her three children. Ruby Mae was the middle child.

My wife and I had married in 1951 and immediately moved three hundred miles away to study for the ministry. Now eleven years had gone by, and I had almost no contact with Ruby Mae in all those years.

My mother had kept us up on the family, somewhat, during that time, and she said that Ruby's life was a mess. She had had two children out of wedlock with a man double her age. They finally got married and had another child, were in financial trouble, and, the last straw, Ruby Mae was involved in a cult.

Because we were taking Mom home in a few days, I agreed to go see Ruby Mae and Ray (her husband) at that time.

What a pleasant surprise our Heavenly Shepherd had for me! When I arrived, only Ruby Mae was home. Ray, a truck driver, was on the road and would not be home for several days. What happened next I have rarely ever witnessed! First, she expressed great joy to see me, so I immediately told her the purpose for my visit. "Ruby Mae, I haven't seen or talked to you in years, but Mom (my mother and her grandmother) has kept me up on what has been taking place in your life. She tells me your life is a mess and to top it all off, you are now involved in a religious cult. The tears began to flow from her eyes and mine.

Her very emotional response was, "But Uncle Jimmie What can I do?"

"Look, you know who Jesus is and that He died for your sins. All you can do is fall down before Him, find forgiveness, and let Him take over. He loves you and wants to do just that."

"You mean right here, right now?"

I replied, "Right here, right now."

Kneeling there in front of the couch, Ruby Mae poured out her heart to the Lord Jesus. No "Repeat after me," No pre-learned, or "Am I doing this right?" type of prayer; just a simple transaction between a guilt ridden sinner and a forgiving Saviour, performed by the Blessed Holy Spirit.

Rising from her knees, her first words were, "I want you to talk to Ray as soon as he gets home."

Unfortunately, I was unable to do that, because we had to travel those three hundred miles back to our home and be there for our Sunday services. Instead, I contacted a pastor friend in that area, told him the situation, and asked him to talk to Ray. He did, and lo and behold, another miracle. Ray, too, responded to our Lord's call to repentance and faith in Him.

For the next year they were active in the local church of the pastor mentioned earlier, busy with two things: trying to make amends for some of their past sins that involved other people (always a good sign of New Life), and growing in the grace and knowledge of their new-found Heavenly Shepherd, the Lord Jesus Christ.

I only saw them once during that year, at which time Ruby Mae handed me the three books she had been studying and using in the short time she had been involved with the cult I mentioned earlier. As she handed them to me she said, "Here, Uncle Jimmie, maybe you can use these to help someone else get free of their deception."

Then the unthinkable happened! Ray developed pneumonia and in a few days died. Now Ruby Mae was a widow with three small children. More than that, they had to move because she could not afford to stay in the house where they had been living. She and the three children moved into a small apartment that didn't even have cupboards in the kitchen.

We had kept our church family abreast of all that was going on in Ruby Mae's life. Although they had never met her, she was regularly in their prayers. Now, after all of these things happened, they wanted to turn their praying into action, asking what they could do to help Ruby Mae. I told them about her need of kitchen cupboards, so they decided to take up an offering and to donate food (mostly canned goods). My family and I then loaded all of those things into our old Ford and went back to Ruby Mae's apartment where I used most of the money to buy materials, built cupboards, and then stocked the shelves with the food they had gathered.

Shortly thereafter, Ruby Mae had one more major thing to face, something that took her and her children more than two thousand miles from home. From the time he was very young; her oldest son had had respiratory problems. The doctors told her that the only thing that might help was to move to a dry climate, so they moved to Mesa, Arizona. From there she sent me a letter, asking a question I had no idea how to answer. She asked, "How do I find a church out here?" Along with that question, she had enclosed three full pages from the local phone book, with several hundred churches listed.

Then there was a second question, asking, "Can you tell me which churches are like the church we attended back home, or is like the church you pastor?"

Now I had a dilemma. With the three pages taken from a phone book containing several hundred church listings, how could I possibly pick out the one(s) that would be a local church(s) where a young widow with three young children could find the help she needed, and more importantly, a new Christian, could find the preaching, teaching, and personal instruction and guidance, to grow into a mature disciple of the Lord with Whom she had so recently entered into a personal relationship?

After a number of calls to those numbers on those telephone book pages Ruby May had sent to me, I gave up going that route. I finally gave her this advice. "Starting with the church nearest you, ask one question: 'Are you a Bible believing church?' If the answer is yes, start attending. If you can determine that Jesus Christ has preeminence in the preaching, teaching, and also in their lives and attitudes, stay there and become one with them in making Christ known. If the church is Christian in doctrine (teaching) only, and love for God, and as well, love for one another are not evident, move on to the next church."

Upon looking back over the description of the church I told Ruby Mae to look for, a very troubling question came to me. <u>Does the church of which I am a pastor fit that</u> <u>description?</u>

About the same time those incidents with Ruby Mae were taking place, some changes were taking place involving our church. A major event that brought about some of those changes was the evening our Sunday school class had a picnic supper on Blueberry Hill (a small picnic area on the State Game Lands). A young farm boy who had grown up in our church had graduated from college and subsequently moved some sixty miles away to take a teaching job. We had invited him and his wife back to speak after our picnic meal. What we heard was anything but uplifting! We gathered around a campfire after several hours of fun, food, and fellowship and were unprepared for what we were about to hear. He opened his presentation by saying, "If we were to move back here, we probably would not attend this church," followed by fifteen minutes of severe criticisms. Everything about the church was bad, from the upkeep of the church building to the condition of the old bus the youth of the church had recently purchased. "It looks like an old migrant farm bus," was the way he described it.

Next, he gave a list of faults about the way the church operated. "A disgrace to God," was the words he chose to use several times to describe the church where he had come to Christ as a young child.

As I listened, I knew there were two questions I had to ask Ed. I liked Ed, and from the first time we met I knew we had one thing in common and that was a sense of humor, but there wasn't any of that coming out of Ed that night.

After Ed finished speaking there was almost near silence. One by one everyone left for home until only Ed, his wife, and I were left. I had waited until that time to ask, "Ed, why did you say all of those things about our church?"

He replied, "I had no intention of saying all that I said, but after I started I thought of so many more things that I see as not being good."

My second question "You have used the phrase, 'Disgrace to God' several times. Did you say all of those negative things because you are concerned for God's Glory?" Ed did not answer.

That night was another one of those sleepless nights as I meditated on those things Ed had said during the "devotional time" that evening. There was truth in many of the things he had said, but I knew that criticism was not the method for making things right or making bad things good. Instead, it generally makes bad things worse, and more times than not, criticism springs from a root of bitterness and ends up defiling others; that is, others apart from the one from whom the criticism originally comes.

Several people came to me over the next week, all with the same attitude, "Who does he think he is, talking about our church like that?"

If I had responded with a similar attitude, there would have been further fractures in this local Body of Christ. Notice I said, "The Body of Christ," which is what a local church is if it is made up of true believers and not merely members of a religious organization that might be labeled as anything from fanatical, fighting fundamentalists, to loose-living liberals. True, a local church is an organization that needs to be cared for well to maintain order, but first and foremost, the church is a living organism and must live and operate with each member drawing its life and power from the Head (Jesus Christ),

33

<u>in order to maintain unity</u>. This is a truth I had known theologically for years, but now, after Ed's speech that night, I, as its pastor and shepherd, would lead this local body where each and every member had been saved by the Grace of God, Who, Himself, had placed each one into that body as it pleased Him (*I CORINTHIANS 12*). Chapter thirteen says that there are three permanent virtues needed to operate a church as a living organism (*FAITH, HOPE, and LOVE*), but the one that is absolutely vital is *LOVE*.

On the night before our Lord went to the Cross, His main concern was for His own to be one with Him and His Father, living in harmony and unity in order to make Him known (*JOHN 17:18-23*). The Glory of God was to be uppermost in the lives of His disciples and be evidenced by their love *"one to another"* (*JOHN 13:34-35*).

From that time on I determined to be a simple country boy, called of God to lead a flock of the Heavenly Shepherd's sheep into the green pastures of His Word, beside the still waters of harmony, unity, rest, and peace, and in the paths of righteousness, all for His Name's sake and the Glory of God.

The morning after Ed's devotional at our class picnic, I walked down to the church building to take a look at "the tropical rain forest entrance" Ed had spoken about. He was right. It looked awful. The vines that covered the sides of the building had grown more than a foot into the entryway. The canopy roof was rotted and leaking, and the short piece of eaves trough and downspout was missing, allowing water to run down onto the walkway leading into the church.

I returned to the parsonage to get my carpentry tools, a ladder, and brush nippers. After a trip to a local lumber company and six hours of labor, "the rain forest entrance" was gone.

The next Sunday, most of the people noticed the change and expressed how nice it looked. I wondered if Ed would notice the difference the next time he and his family came for a Sunday visit.

There was only one negative comment. One person said, "Who ruined the nice vines over the entryway? I liked them."

By the way, Ruby Mae never did find the kind of church I had described to her, but some way or another, the Heavenly Shepherd did see her through all of her difficulties, and gave her another husband and another child. Then, three years ago my granddaughter Hannah, my wife and I made a trip to a small desert town in Arizona where she lives with her aging husband and forty some year old daughter who helps take care of them. She (the daughter) drives forty miles each way, to another small desert town, where she teaches in a grade school.

Having never met my wife or me, her first words, when she saw us, were, "Uncle Jimmie, I've looked forward to meeting you. Mom has told me so much about you. She said you led her to Jesus. She led me to Jesus, and all I want to do is lead the children I teach to Jesus." Down inside I cried (what joy)!

As for Ed, after several years as a school teacher, he moved back into the area and went back to farming and, yes, he came back to the church with which he had found so many faults two years before. Even so, he had been right about many of the things he had said that night on Blueberry Hill, and God had used him to begin to make some changes in my ministry, starting with "the rain forest entrance" into the church building. I could fix that myself. The other things that needed some fixing were people. Only God could do that, and He did, beginning with Ed and myself.

He and I had many more discussions and also some serious confrontations over the next six years I was his pastor. His critical spirit did not end with his speech to us on Blueberry Hill. When something was not right, or Ed perceived that something was not right (including me), I was going to hear about it, and in no uncertain terms. But you know through each confrontation God was working in both of us. Ed was learning that longsuffering, gentleness and meekness were key elements in the fruit of Gods Spirit who dwelt in both of us and I was learning the power of soft answers coupled with God given patience.

We both knew the bond that made us one was an eternal bond. That bond was and still is forty plus years later the person of Jesus Christ. We are members of His Body. Earthly relationships change and ultimately end, including memberships in the local church as an organization, not so with the relationship God brought us into through His Sons death, burial and resurrection. That is a vital relationship <u>He performs</u>. It brings each one into an eternal relationship with not only Himself, but also with one another. That is the oneness our Lord talked with His Heavenly Father about in John 17. We are members of a Body that has the same Head which is Jesus Christ. I can only rejoice.

As for Ruby Mae, she is still my niece and I am still Uncle Jimmie, but that relationship too will end. The relationship she entered into that day beside the couch made us a brother and sister in Christ, a relationship that has no end.

Transformed lives, branches in the Heavenly Vine, still bearing fruit for Gods glory. That is who we all are: Ruby Mae, her daughter, Ed and myself. We all know we are not all we shall be, but we all know God is still working in us, along with all those He has reached through us over the past forty five plus years. His Word, believed, obeyed and given out brings forth abiding fruit.

It was through these two incidents that happened over the same period of time where God taught me that a local church must operate first and foremost as a living organism drawing life from Him and secondly as an organization. Operating as a Living Organism with each member drawing life from our Living Head is absolutely necessary to maintain unity, and grow spiritually.

The result is a local church that is some what like the one I told Ruby Mae to look for in Phoenix all those years ago; a church where Faith, Hope and Love abound, evidenced by transformed lives. That is lives God continues to fix. (Sanctify)

Won't it be great when the fixing is all done and *He presents us unto Himself a glorious church not having spot, or wrinkle, or any such thing? Then we shall be holy and without blemish. (Eph. 5:27)* Until then let us pray for one another as He prayed to The Father for us. *"Sanctify them through thy truth, Thy WORD IS TRUTH."* *(Jn. 17:17)*

A HOME UNDER ATTACK

Weldon and Lindy

It was past midnight. My wife and I had just gotten to sleep when the doorbell began to ring violently. Then there came a persistent pounding and a man's voice.

As quickly as possible, I jumped out of bed, pulled my pants on, ran down the stairs, taking them three at a time, while the pounding on the door continued. I quickly unlocked and opened the door. There stood Weldon. "Pastor! Pastor! I need help!" were his first words. "My wife is trying to kill herself. She just swallowed a whole bottle of pills. I don't know what they were, but she's out of her mind."

Within minutes, we were at his home with Lindy moaning and muttering words that, for the most part, were not understandable. Weldon and I managed to get her out of the house and into the back seat of my car. Traveling a lot faster than I should have been, we soon reached the hospital emergency room entrance. By this time, Lindy was nearly limp and there weren't any understandable words, just some moans and the sound of, "Oh!! Oh!! Oh!!!

Her last words, on the way to the hospital, that I could understand, were weak, but audible. As near as I could make them out, here is what I heard. "It won't be long now, and you'll not have to put up with me anymore." I assumed those words were meant for her husband who was trying to keep her awake until we got her to the doctors at the hospital.

I can't imagine the pain he was feeling through all this time and the hours that followed, as we sat there waiting for someone to come through those emergency room doors with news; good or bad.

When we sat down in that waiting room I prayed, and then there was total silence. Neither one of us spoke. We both knew the circumstances that had led up to this climactic incident. Going through my mind were thoughts of former times when I had sat with others in this and other waiting rooms, wondering what words we would hear when the nurse or doctor entered, from either an emergency or operating room door.

Only a few months before this, a similar incident had taken place. In that case, the parents of a college age daughter had found her unconscious in her bedroom. She had overdosed on drugs. It was nearly two days of waiting in her case. I was not there the entire two days, but members of that family were, and the pain of those two days was still present in my mind. In that situation, she did pull through, but the results of it, her parents and I were still dealing with months later. I wondered and prayed, recalling that incident. What kind of news would we soon get about Lindy?

Let's return to what I meant when I said, "Weldon and I both knew what had led up to this climactic incident." My wife and I were suspicious that something was just not right in Weldon and Lindy's lives after they invited us to go along to a banquet with them, several months before. It was nearly an hour's drive to the banquet. We had not traveled far when Weldon asked, "Pastor, what are you teaching the senior youth?"

I was the senior youth leader as well as the pastor all our ten years in that pastorate. "The Bible," was my response.

With that he continued, "Yeah, I know that, but what I mean is, what specifically are you teaching now? Are you talking to them about sex?"

I answered with a little humor in my voice, saying, "Yes I am. There's a lot about sex in God's Word."

His next question was, "Did you tell them you would answer any question they asked you in the area of sex, if any of them would come to you individually? Our son told us you said that."

(Their son, Darin, was one of the younger boys in our mixed, senior youth group.)

I took the next five minutes to explain what had taken place at our Bible study the week before, and here is a brief summary of what I told Weldon and Lindy that night.

"We are studying *MATTHEW, Chapter 1,* where we have the account of Christ's birth, which we know in Theology, as 'The Virgin Birth.' I'm sure you are familiar with that scripture. One of the youths asked, 'What does it mean, in verse eight when it says about Mary and Joseph, *before they came together?'*

"Some of the older youths snickered when that question was asked. I answered the question by simply saying that they hadn't had any sexual relations before Christ was born. Then I referred to *verses 24 and 25,* where it says, *'Joseph took unto him his wife and knew her not till she had brought forth her firstborn son.'* Those words *'knew her not'* mean the same thing.

"The next question was, 'What do you mean by sex relations?'

"With many of the group snickering under their breath at that question and a few more that followed, I made this statement to the whole group, 'You go home and ask your parents for answers to your questions in this area. If they won't answer them, come to me one on one, and I will answer them for you.'"

It was then that Weldon said, "We just wanted to know what you are teaching the youth group. After last week's study, Darin came home and immediately said, 'If you won't answer my questions, I know who will. Pastor Walter said that I can go to him and he will answer **any question I ask him.**'"

There wasn't any more conversation (comments or questions) involving the area of sex, for the remainder of our evening together, but there would be in the very near future.

Arriving home that night, both my wife and I thought that the main reason they had invited us to that banquet was to ask me about what had happened at the youth Bible study the week before. We also felt that they were not very happy with the way the questions asked, were answered. Neither of us was sure how they took my explanation, either.

Several weeks passed by. I had installed a basketball hoop at the end of the blacktop parking lot. There were several boys who regularly came to play, and Darin was one of them. He and I was a pretty even match at that time.

After one of those strenuous games of one on one, Darin, with tears in his eyes, said, "Dad and Mom aren't getting along. I'm afraid one of them is going to leave." We talked for fifteen or twenty minutes and parted, both of us feeling sad. Another night, just lying in bed for hours, meditating, praying, thinking, and yes, worrying about what was going to happen to Weldon and his family.

This calling to care for the Heavenly Shepherd's flock, surely involves many sleepless hours and sometimes, sleepless nights. Other than pray, what else is there to do until the Heavenly Shepherd Himself intervenes or gives explicit instructions?

Several weeks later, He did intervene. In the middle of an afternoon, our doorbell rang. This time it was Lindy. She was crying, and I could tell she had been crying for some time. I invited her in and for fifteen or twenty minutes, she poured her heart out, like I have heard few people ever do. I will recall her words, as nearly as I can.

Sitting there on our couch with a handful of tissues, holding her head between her hands, and with tears flowing freely, she said, "Weldon's going to leave us (her and their children). He's going to leave us. I'm going to lose my home and it is all my fault, it is all my fault. He's been so good to me, never anything but good to me, but I can't love him back. I try but I just don't have any romantic feelings of any kind anymore. I have been this way for years, and he has put up with it until now. Several weeks ago I was told that Weldon is seeing a woman where he works. He doesn't deny it but says they are only friends, and they just eat lunch together in the cafeteria where they work.

"I don't want to lose him. I don't want to lose my home (tears and more tears flow freely). Why? Oh, why can't I be a wife to him? I love him, and I know he loves me, too. I'm so mixed up. I'm just so mixed up."

Next, she told me that something had been happening to her ever since she had heard of her husband's interest in the woman where he worked. Again, these are her own words, as nearly as I can recollect, about this crazy thing that was taking place inside of her.

I listened as she said, "I'm embarrassed to even talk about this. It's just awful. Ever since Weldon admitted he was having lunch with a co-worker, I'm...No! I can't say it! It's too awful!"

My response was, "What is it?"

She then continued, "It's awful! I'm beginning to have these romantic feelings I haven't had for years, but they are toward another person, other than Weldon."

I asked, "Are you and this man involved romantically in any way?"

"Oh! No! No!" she replied. "He just works near me. He has no idea I'm experiencing these feelings toward him.

"Oh, I'm so mixed up! Why can't I be toward my husband as I know I should be?"

With the promise that I would talk to Weldon at the first opportunity, we prayed, seeking God's wisdom, and then she walked out the door. Again, more sleepless hours, seeking what to say when I did get to talk with Weldon.

Saturday morning was men's basketball at the high school gym. I knew Weldon was nearly always there, and sure enough, in he came, just a bit late.

For two hours, twenty of us alternated on four-five man teams. Running the full length of that gym, we were all dead tired.

When Weldon said he was going home to take his shower, I said, "How about stopping at the church for a few minutes. I have something I would like to talk about." I am sure he was aware of what I wanted to talk about, and he seemed more than willing.

We sat across the aisle from each other, in the back pews. I began by telling him of his son's fears about his father and mother separating. Then I spoke of his wife's coming to the parsonage a few days before. I was absolutely honest and told him all both had said to me. He acknowledged that everything his wife had said to me was true and was deeply touched by his son's fears.

When I asked him about his relationship with the woman he worked with, he assured me that eating lunch together in the cafeteria was the extent of that relationship. He admitted that if he allowed it to go any further, he probably would lose his position as well as his family. Then I added, "Worse than that, you'd disgrace the Lord you believe in and claim you love." With that, we departed to our homes, to take those badly needed showers.

After that meeting, I began to see a ray of hope in the whole situation. I honestly believed all three, Weldon, Lindy, and their son, wanted the same thing for their family. The younger children were too young to understand what was happening, but were still feeling some of the pain.

What should I do? I knew where and what the main issues were. Here was a family in turmoil. There was a wife and mother near a break-down, with emotions neither she, her husband, nor I could understand. Then, there was a son who had little on his mind other than thoughts and fears about what was going to happen between Dad and Mom, and a frustrated husband and father who was faced by a temptation of which he clearly knew that if he yielded to it, what the consequences would be.

Something had to be done, and soon, if this family was to remain intact. I saw the situation as an assault of the Evil One to destroy a Christian family and disgrace God's name.

To this point, there was a lot of hurting, frustration, fear, and temptation. No one had made a choice to do the wrong thing, but emotions were near the breaking point. The pressures on both Weldon and Lindy were nearly unbearable. I knew that the only solution was for both to hear and understand what God says in His Word about oneness in the marriage bond. They needed to understand that God made us sexual beings (male and female). They needed to understand that sex within their marriage bond was God-given and God- ordained.

There is all of this and so many more related topics and questions to which we find instructions and answers in God's Word. For the last fifty years I have made these things a large part of pre-marital counseling. To understand and make right choices before hand is a whole lot easier than getting out of the consequences brought on by wrong ones.

In both the prayer our Heavenly Shepherd taught His disciples in *MATTHEW 6:13*, and the prayer He prayed for His disciples in

JOHN 17:15, we learn His desire for His own is to be kept from sin and the Evil One.

To this point, the Evil One had only succeeded in harassing Weldon and Lindy. Would they understand and get their marriage (especially the sexual aspect of it) together before it was too late? The subject of divorce, that God says He hates (*MALACHI 2:16*), was now in the picture.

As an under-shepherd, caring for the Heavenly Shepherd's flock, what more was I to do to help Weldon and Lindy before Satan's snare slammed shut on their marriage and home *(JAMES 1:14 and 15)?*

All I could do was pray and to wait for God to reveal my next move, and it wasn't long in coming. It was just a few days after Weldon and I talked, after the Saturday morning basketball, and after midnight, that Weldon came to our door in a panic. That brings us back to the waiting room, waiting for news about Lindy from the emergency room staff.

Nearly an hour had passed, in complete silence. A door opened and a doctor came over to us. A wave of relief swept over us when we heard the doctor say, "Lindy's going to be all right." Then he went on to say, "She's going to have a sore stomach for a few days. She swallowed a bottle of aspirin. We are going to keep her here for several hours, and then you can take her home."

Weldon and I waited those few hours, during which we talked about the days and months ahead. Without going into details, those days and months were a time of growing in understanding of God's plans and instructions for having a mutually satisfying husband and wife relationship that glorifies our God Who made us *"male and female."* That relationship continues to this day, many, many years later.

This is another example of "a bad thing that didn't happen" (no divorce, no broken home, three children that were not torn apart in the process, and best of all, their Saviour, the Heavenly Shepherd, did not have to go through the grief and disgrace of several of His sheep going astray). God had kept a family from the Evil One, and none of the flock even knew that family was under attack by that *"Roaring Lion, who goes about seeking whom he might devour."*

What a privilege to be a co-worker with God and watch Him fix this home before it was beyond repair.

A short time before the Evil One attacked Weldon's and Lindy's home, two incidents took place in my home; one at the breakfast table, and one the evening before.

From the time my father died in 1955 until my mother died in 1971, she always spent a month or two with us each summer. Those were special times for our whole family. My wife loved her as her own mother, and our children thought Grandma was the greatest. We all loved her homemade bread, pies, and cookies, too.

She and I had many conversations, recalling things from the past, during her stays with us over the last sixteen years of her life. One of those conversations took place at the breakfast table. When she came to breakfast that morning, I could see she had something on her mind, and I could tell it was something she had done a lot of thinking about.

There wasn't much conversation during the meal. She was especially quiet until she abruptly said, "Jimmy, what were you talking to that couple about, last night?"

With a smile, I answered just as abruptly, "Their sex life, Mom."

With my reply, Mom's face turned the prettiest red I had ever seen for she was totally embarrassed. She was past seventy years old and taken completely off guard by my answer. She remained speechless for a moment, and then said, "That's what I thought I heard you talking to that young couple about. I couldn't believe I was hearing right."

Well, you know, she wasn't supposed to be hearing our conversation at all, and how she did is still beyond me. Let me explain. I had made an appointment to talk to this couple who were having marital problems. They had come to the parsonage, rather than me going to their home.

At that time, our children were young (six and two years of age). They, along with my wife and mother, stayed in the recreational room and we met in the living room. Between the recreational room and the living room there were three archways (one between the living room and dining room, one between the dining room and the kitchen, and one off to the left, between the kitchen and the recreational room). With the children playing and my wife and mother conversing, there isn't any way anyone could possibly hear our counseling session, or so I thought. I was wrong! Mom heard just enough bits and pieces of our conversation to give her a restless night, thinking about what she thought she had heard.

Mom continued, saying, "I've never heard of a minister talking about such things."

My response to my wonderful, blushing mother was a question. "Why do you suppose that is?"

"Well, you just don't talk about those things," was all she could say.

"Mom, sex and money are the two main causes of problems within homes today, and God's Word has a lot to say about both of them.

"It has been my experience in the few, short years that I have been an under-shepherd, that ignorance or disobedience as to what God's Word teaches in these two areas (especially the sexual area) causes more divisions in Christians' homes than all other areas combined."

I continued, with a broad grin on my face, and her face still red with embarrassment, by asking several questions. "Mom, while we are on the subject, let me ask you a question. 'Why didn't you or Dad ever say anything to us (my brother or me) about sex?'"

My mother replied, "Didn't your Dad ever talk to you about THIS SUBJECT?" (She still couldn't use the word, sex).

My answer was a gentle, calm, "No."

"Are you sure? He always said he was going to talk to you when he had a chance."

In a flash of insight, I said, "I take that back. One Sunday afternoon, as I was about to go out to see Doris (my girlfriend then, and my wife now, for over fifty-seven years), Dad said, 'Come here, Jimmy. I want to talk to you.' He was sitting in his chair in the living room, by the radio.

As I was on my way out the door, I came back inside, went over to where he was sitting, and asked, 'Yes, Dad, what is it?' I could see he was struggling for words to say, so I asked a second time, 'What is it, Dad?'

"His exact words were, 'You and Doris are seeing a lot of each other. Just behave yourself.'

"I responded by asking, 'What do you mean by behave myself?'"

"He said, 'I'm not saying any more. Just behave yourself.'"

"I tried one more time to get him to explain himself, getting the same response."

I then looked at Mom's sweet, blushing face and humorously said, "Yes Mom, that was the extent of my verbal sex education from Dad, and you know what? He had as much trouble talking to me way back then, as you are having now." We both laughed.

We then spent most of that morning talking about all of the situations we were both aware of where families and relationships were badly marred and some completely destroyed by the misuse and/or misunderstanding of sex.

The sum and substance of our conversation that morning so many years ago, was this young pastor teaching his seventy year-old mother what God has to say about sex, although, he didn't teach her anything she didn't already know. They were just things she and his father should have taught him fifteen to twenty years before, but were too embarrassed to talk about "such things."

In reality, they were the things I taught the couple the night before, the same Truths from God's Word that freed Weldon and Lindy, so they could love one another as God intended when He ordained the marriage union from the creation of man and woman in *GENESIS, Chapters 1 and 2.* (A marriage created by Him for His Glory, and a greater picture of the union between His Son and His Bride, the Church, both of which His Arch Enemy has been out to deceive, divide, and destroy ever since their institution by and for Him).

"Marriage is honorable among all, and the bed undefiled;
but fornicators and adulterers God will judge,"
(HEBREWS 11:4).

THROUGH TERRIBLE
HURT AND HEARTACHE
" Only You LORD Can Ever Possibly Fix This Home"

Lennie and Dottie

"**P**astor, somebody better talk to Lennie, and soon. We just came from his place and things are NOT GOOD!"

Those were the words from Lennie's brother and sister in law. The fact was, I had talked with Lennie more than a dozen times over the last two months. It had been that long since Lennie's wife had run off with another man. I mentioned that incident in my previous book, "Fifty Years a Country Pastor." In that book I told how this totally frustrated, young pastor sought advice from a pastor I highly admired for his wisdom coupled with extreme humility. His words to me back then were, "Jim you're putting too much of this load on yourself. The church you are pastoring does not belong to you. It belongs to the Lord who purchased it with His Own blood. Just turn all of these things you are telling me over to Him. Then, to the best of your ability, do what He says about each situation, leaving the results up to Him. **After all, only He can change peoples' hearts and make things right.**"

Searching the Scriptures and praying day and night, I was trying to follow Dr. Griffis's advice.

Day after day I was trying to give Lennie the advice and support he needed, while at the same time trying to give support to those in the church who could not understand how a thing like this could happen to a couple who were looked upon as two of the most spiritual leaders in this small flock. It was also the talk of the community.

"Is Dottie back home with Lennie, or is she off with that 'Tramp' again?" That was the question I was asked time and again ever since Dottie got up and left the evening service to run away with "that Tramp."

For two months, again and again, she had either gone with "that Tramp" or she was home with Lennie. To make matters worse, "that Tramp" was a married man living with his wife (or so we thought at the time). We were to find out later that the woman he was living with was not his wife, but another married woman who had left her husband for "that Tramp." We also discovered that he had broken up another young couple by having an affair with the young wife, just six months earlier. To top it all off, he had a wife and several children in a state several hundred miles away. All of this was found out when this whole scenario reached a climax less than a year later.

I immediately went to see Lennie. When I arrived, he was sitting on the front porch with a high- powered rifle across his knees. I just sat down on the front edge of the porch, waiting for him to say the first words. By nature he was a soft-spoken person. His first words: " I am just going to wait until they (his wife and the Tramp)come over that hill, pick them both off (kill them), and then shoot myself."

My reply, what I believe was a God-given response, was, "Yeah Lennie that would solve the whole situation. Christ would be honored, the church problem would be gone, and your two children would grow up and be able to say, 'Mommy did a bad thing when she left us for another man, but Daddy solved it. He just shot Mommy and that bad man and then killed himself, leaving us alone to grow up with none of those horrible problems.'"

"I guess I'm not thinking too straight, am I," were his only words. Then he took the gun back into the house, came back out, and sitting there on the porch, broke down and cried. When he had calmed down a bit, between sobs, he said, "I can't take any more. I just can't take any more. Something has to be done."

I knew he was right. Something had to be done. At that time, all I could say to Lennie was, "Let's continue to pray for wisdom to know what to do and for strength for you to endure this horrible betrayal." Then I added, "And let's pray for Dottie, that somehow she will come to her senses."

The next question was, could Lennie take Dottie back, even if she came back home for good? Time would show that the worst was yet to come, but before we delve into that, we need to go back and fill in some blanks. I could not continue to tell the church, Lennie, or even myself, "Let's just pray about it," for I was all prayed out, advised out, and explained out, and I wanted out! My wife was even more exasperated than I.

Let's go back to the night Dottie ran off with this man, several months before. Lennie and I just could not believe she did this of her own will. She must have been drugged, blackmailed, or kidnapped, was our only reasoning. The next morning we reported her to the police as a missing person, but when we told them the whole story of her disappearance, they were not very concerned. I have since found out that events like this are commonplace with police departments, and most of those who run away do so of their own volition. Not many are coerced.

When we discovered that the police were not very concerned, we went to a nearby city and hired a private detective to look for Dottie.

Each evening from that Sunday on was spent with Lennie and his two young children, waiting for news from Dottie. We heard nothing Monday, nothing Tuesday, and nothing on Wednesday. Then, Thursday evening about 11 p.m. car lights appeared over the knoll above the farm house. The car stopped about two hundred feet up the road and someone got out. The car backed up to the top of the knoll, turned around, and disappeared into the darkness.

At first we did not recognize the person coming down the road. It appeared to be a woman wearing a full-length fur coat. She came right up to the porch steps and in through the open door. It was Dottie, but she surely did not look like the Dottie I knew. The Dottie I knew was a plain, graying, forty year old farm wife. This woman in the long fur coat had bracelets on both arms (one engraved with the names Dottie and Fran), several rings on her fingers, and to top it all off, she was a beautiful brunette. Her first words were aimed at me. She said, "I thought I would get a lecture when I got home, but I didn't think it would be until tomorrow morning."

The next words were spoken by Lennie who bluntly asked, "Dottie, why didn't you just die?"

Dottie replied, "Lennie, don't talk like that."

I interrupted calmly, "Come on Dottie, I want to talk to you."

We went into the next room, and I closed the door. I then asked, "Dottie, what's going on?" I didn't have to say anything more, because for the next ten to fifteen minutes she let me know exactly what was going on inside her and that it did not just happen over the past few days.

In a condensed version, she said, "I hate this farm. Lennie and I were married thirteen years ago and we have not been away from this farm for even one night in all those years, except two times to have our babies. I've begged Lennie to take a vacation, but he says he doesn't need one, and beside that, he can't. He has to milk his darned cows twice a day. I hate them, too. He doesn't get in from taking care of those cows until nine or sometimes ten o'clock, and by then, most times, the children are in bed. More times than not, he just socks himself down in that overstuffed chair and falls asleep. There he is until the next morning, and by the time I'm awake, he's back out to the barn doing chores.

"I've had it! I decided years ago that I would take the first opportunity I got to get away from this place. I didn't expect it would be a man that would offer me that opportunity, but that's the way it happened."

Then I asked her my second question, "Where is the Lord in all of this?"

Her reply: "That's what I said to you when I came in the door. Now comes the lecture."

After listening to her for those ten or fifteen minutes, I felt more sorry for, than disgusted with her. (This scenario, with some variations, I would hear many times over the next forty-eight years. Fortunately, most cases do not end up with one or the other party making a life-altering decision).

50

When you read the case of Weldon and Lindy previously in this book, you saw what God intended to happen before things got so bad.

I went home late that night, wondering what would happen next. Was Dottie home for good? Could Lennie forgive her? What about "the Tramp?" Would he go back to his wife (The one whom we thought was his wife at the time)?

Two days went by, and it was about eight o'clock Saturday evening when a car pulled up in front of the parsonage, with its horn blowing. Going outside, even though it was quite dark, I could see the hand of a man motioning me to come to him. It was Fran, "the Tramp." He had an envelope in his hand, and I could see that he was crying. I opened the passenger side door and sat down next to him. With tears running down his cheeks he managed to spill out, "I've done a terrible thing. I've destroyed a good family and I'm so sorry. I want to tell God I'm sorry. I've gone all over three towns trying to find a priest. I can't even find a church that isn't locked, where I can pray. I just want to tell God how sorry I am and beg his forgiveness."

I explained to him that he did not have to be in a church to pray, and how God would hear and forgive him. Then I told him that Christ died for our sins and would forgive all his sins if he would but repent and believe personally in Jesus Christ.

He did pray, but his prayer was not one of submission to the Saviour. Rather, it was for deliverance from the **guilt** that was preying on his mind, not deliverance from **the sin** that caused his guilt (I've seen this happen so many times over the years. Satan is so subtle. **So often I have seen those who want to be freed from the consequences of sin, of which guilt is one, while continuing in the sin that caused the guilt).**

Fran then handed me the envelope he had in his hand, with this explanation), "Here is four hundred dollars, the money left over from the spree Dottie and I had in New York City. I want you to give it to Lennie."

They had cashed in Dottie's life insurance policy of several thousand dollars and spent all of it except the four hundred dollars the envelope contained. With a promise that he was leaving that part of the county and that we would not hear from him again, he drove away.

I could hardly wait until the next morning to tell Lennie what I thought was good news. He and his two children were present in Sunday School and the morning service, but not Dottie. Of course, I really did not expect to see her there as several people in the church knew what she had done, and she would not want to face them.

Lennie waited until the church emptied, after the morning service. I handed him the envelope and told him to open it. As he counted the money, he looked at me and exclaimed, "What's this!"

I explained about Fran's visit the evening before. I could see in his verbal response and his facial expressions, emotions of anger, disgust, fear, depression, and a mixture of hate and happiness, (if all of those are possible) t one time. The fact that Fran had returned the remaining money did seem to give him a ray of hope that the worst was over. I knew that underneath it all, there was a part of him that wanted her back, but, at the same time, he knew that everything could not be the same.

I wondered what the results would be when he faced Dottie about the money, because they were poor people and that life insurance policy was her life's savings.

Fifteen minutes later, none of these things mattered. As I walked in the door of the parsonage, the phone was ringing. It was Lennie. "She's gone again!" was all he said.

As it turned out, Dottie and Fran had this all arranged. When Lennie and the children had gone to church, Fran came and picked her up.

What was the meaning of Fran's visit with me the evening before? I never did figure that out and never got an opportunity to ask him about it, as I never saw him again. It was not that he was not around, because he was constantly coming to pick Dottie up, and in a few days, bring her back. This had happened four or five times over those two months that followed that Sunday evening when she had left the first time.

It was all this coming and going that led up to that day when Lennie was sitting on his porch with the high-powered rifle across his knees, the same day he declared, "I can't take it anymore. I just can't take it any more. Something must be done."

During those two months I had talked to Dottie several times. My first approach was as a spiritual brother trying to restore one who was *"...overtaken in a fault..."* according to God's instruction in *GALATIANS 5:1.* I soon discovered that Dottie was more than just *"...one overtaken in a fault..."* Her affair with Fran continued, and to her, it had become **no big deal**. In fact, throughout all of this, she attended church services several times, but there were no signs of repentance.

Lennie was right when he had said, "Something has to be done." He was willing to forgive her the first time, but incapable of living with the continuing situation. I was fully aware of the teaching of Scripture in such a situation, as it relates to the Church Body and knew that something had to be done.

When I explained to the church board what we needed to do, they were in agreement. According to *I CORINTHIANS 5,* we (the church body) needed to totally withdraw fellowship from Dottie, so at the next meeting of the Church Body, we voted to do just that. This was my first experience with "Church Discipline," and I was about to have a learning experience that could never be learned from any book.

First, even though it was made clear to the church body that God's Word says (*I CORINTHIANS 5:4-13*) that the discipline is withdrawal of fellowship, there were those who believed that merely meant removing Dottie's name from the membership roll.

Second, even though God's Word is clear, there were those who felt it was not our business to judge anyone else.

Explain as I would, there were those who believed that what others did was between them and God. Scriptures like *"Judge not that ye be not judged"* and *"Vengeance is mine sayeth the Lord"* were quoted over and over again to counteract God's Instructions for "church discipline." One person even quoted the words of Jesus in *John 8:7*: *"He that is without sin among you, let him cast the first stone,"* to show his unworthiness to participate in "church discipline."

Third, and the most difficult to explain, was the open arms of a neighboring pastor. I have found out, through the years, that there are always those local churches and pastors who will welcome anyone into "their" flock, but in this case it was even worse, for this pastor criticized us for being unloving and mean-spirited for what we had done to Dottie. He gave no thought to what she had done and continued to do to the Lord's Name, her husband, children, the church's testimony, and to herself as well.

After talking to that pastor, Dottie became angry with me. In her heart, she knew that the majority of us who were disciplining her by refusing to fellowship with her, truly loved her.

During my last visit with her, I had her read what God says to His children who go astray. *"Whom the Lord loves He chastens, and scourges every son whom He receives," (HEBREWS 12:6),* and the entire passage of *HEBREWS 12:1-17.* I also reminded her of the prodigal son, who had to *"come to the end of himself"* before returning home. When he did, in repentance, return to his Father and home, he found a waiting Father, with open arms *(LUKE 15:11-24).* I assured her that she would find the same to be true if she was truly His child, and as well with us, whom that pastor had called "unloving and mean-spirited."

One Sunday I wrote a short article entitled, **"Who Suffered Most: The Wayward Prodigal or the Waiting Father?",** and put it in the church bulletin. I was sure I knew the answer back then. Fifty years later, I know I know the answer, and anyone who loves with God's Love also knows.

There is no pain worse than **"betrayed love."** My Saviour knew all about that the night before His trip up Golgotha's Hill, and I am sure that some of you who are reading this know what I am talking about as well.

Now, let's return to the statement I made earlier, that the final blow had not yet fallen. That blow came some months later, when Dottie had left home permanently. For some time, we were not sure where she was. It turned out that she had moved in with Fran and the woman we thought was his wife. The three of them lived together in a small trailer on a back country road. During this time,

Dottie and Millie (the other woman) had babies within three weeks of each other.

After all of this, could Lennie, Dottie, and their two children ever be a family again? When I left pastoring that church, I would have said it was impossible, but actually, this was not the end of the story. Several years later, early one morning, my telephone rang. It was Dottie. Now I am not sure how she got our new telephone number as we had moved to a new pastorate some three years before. Her first words were, "Pastor, Lennie and I have gotten our lives straightened out with the Lord and are back together. We have moved to this new town and I just wanted to tell you that I am sorry for all the trouble I caused you and the church back there five years ago. Also, we (Lennie and Dottie) would like you and Doris to come visit us. We both thank you for all you have done for us."

We did visit them several times over the next several years. They were truly a united family again. They later moved to a mid-western state and a member of their family told me that they lived together as a family until Lennie died, some twenty-five years later.

I also had contact with another member of that family about eighteen years after all of this had transpired. I had been invited to speak at a high school graduation banquet. When I arrived, a beautiful young lady came up to me and said, "Pastor Walter, you don't know me, my name is Penny B. My mother told me you are a godly man and that I should listen closely to all you have to say." That young lady was the baby Dottie had out of wedlock with Fran. Lennie had taken her in when he and Dottie had reconciled and raised and loved her as his own child, though she retained Fran's name. Only one filled with God's Love could possibly forgive and see his family restored. *God is truly busy fixing things*. In this case a home I would have said was beyond repair.

This is just another illustration of the struggles that go on even in the lives of those who profess to be followers of Jesus Christ. Christ's Arch Enemy is always there to lead them astray. Blessed is the Local Church that has those humble enough to ("*in lowliness of mind esteem others better than themselves*" where "*THEY LOOK NOT ONLY AFTER THEIR OWN INTERESTS, BUT AFTER THE INTERESTS OF OTHERS*").

Doubly blessed is the flock that has a shepherd like Timothy, whom Paul described as *"one who will naturally care for the flock's state, while so many seek their own interests, not the things that are Jesus Christ's" (PHILIPPIANS chapter 2, especially verses 3-4 and 19-21).*

It was another faithful co-laborer with God, who, though faithful counsel from God's Word, brought Lennie and Dottie back together. Using the analogy of sowing and reaping: *"Some sow, some water,* ***GOD GIVES THE INCREASE." (I COR.3:6)*** That faithful servant and I have rejoiced together more than once over the miracle God performed in the reunion of that impossible situation. God truly is busy fixing things.

A HOME PRESERVED BY GODS FORGIVENESS AND CLEANSING

"Neither do I condemn thee, go and sin no more"
JOHN 8:11b

Cham and Minnie

While I was trying to deal with all the fallout from the Lennie and Dottie situation, along came another. Cham, a highly respected man in the church, was unloading a load of firewood he had cut for us. During that time, he did not say one word, which was unusual for him. It was evident that something was bothering him. When we had the firewood unloaded, he would have left without speaking to me, had I not asked, "What's the matter, Cham?"

He blurted out, "Pastor, we have another Dottie to KICK OUT of the church!"

"What are you talking about, Cham? We did not KICK Dottie OUT of the church!"

"Well, whatever we did, we have to do it to another person," he protested.

"Who are you talking about?" I inquired.

"My wife! That's who!" he exclaimed. With tears running down his cheeks and his voice quivering, he continued, "I just found out what has been going on two days ago, and I haven't slept since. For the past month, Minnie and my boss have been having an affair."

"Are you sure about that?" I asked him.

"Yes I'm sure," he replied, "she wants a divorce and says Del wants to divorce his wife, too, and then they can get married."

"She actually said that to you?"

"Yeah, she said that, and if I hadn't walked away, I don't know what I might have done."

"Do you still love Minnie?"

"When she told me all of this I could have said I hated her, but right now I'm not sure. I can't imagine what will happen to Sam, Shawn, and Debbie (their three children) if she leaves us. I know I love those three kids."

"I'll be over to talk to you and Minnie tonight, after I am sure your children have gone to bed and are asleep, around ten o'clock. Don't tell Minnie I am coming, and do not tell her that you have talked to me about any of this."

"That's okay with me," he replied. I had prayer with him and he left.

I went inside and told my wife about this new wrinkle in our ministry. Again, I heard the same thing I heard after the whole thing with Lennie and Dottie, "Let's get out of here." She had first spoken those words to me the day we had moved into this pastorate several years before. That was the day she over-heard three women who were helping us move in, crying. They were crying because they could not stand the thought of Joe and Sandra (the former pastor and his wife) being gone.

I would hear those words several more times before we did leave to tend another of the Heavenly Shepherd's flocks. I knew exactly what she was feeling, for at that time, I was feeling the same way, but how could I run away when I believed I was there because God had put me there?

She asked one more question, to which I did not have the answer, "What are you going to say when you go over to Cham's and Minnie's tonight?" Then she added, "You know how I hate to be here alone at night."

Into our bedroom I went to cry out to my Heavenly Shepherd for wisdom, understanding, and strength, to know what I would say to Minnie and Cham that night. There was no way I wanted to go through another long, drawn out affair like we had been going through with Lennie and Dottie for months.

Leaving my wife there alone with our year old daughter at 9:30 P.M. was not easy for them or me, especially on a cold winter night.

This was only one of hundreds of such nights a co-laborer with Gods' wife lives through. Few people understand the difficult, lonely life of a pastor's wife. Night after night is filled with Bible studies, counseling sessions and meetings of all kinds, playing sports with the young people, emergencies, and trying to rescue straying sheep, which is what I would be doing this night until one o'clock in the morning. It would be a night no one of the flock would ever know about except Cham, Minnie, my wife, and myself.

My wife is a worrier, especially when those nights are snowy, slippery nights or difficult and sometimes dangerous domestic situations. For years, I reprimanded her for that worrying instead of being sympathetic. It took years for me to understand that there are a lot of genetically inherited traits as well as habits, deeply ingrained since childhood, that we all have (some good and some bad). Worrying is one of hers and a sense of humor is one of mine (good until carried too far or expressed at the wrong time, both of which I have been guilty more than once) during all those years in the pastorate.

At 9:30 p.m., I went over those snowy, back, dirt roads to see Cham and Minnie. I did not know it at the time, but I was about to witness God perform a miracle. The following is a condensed version of a battle between God and Satan over a marriage and a family. Satan was there to deceive, divide, and destroy that home. God was there to defend and deliver two, whom he had made one, from sin and Satan's subtle snare.

As I said at the beginning of this book, there are two institutions God has ordained; the home and the Church. From day one of their institution, Satan has determined to destroy both and thereby disgrace God.

Minnie met me at the door with this greeting, "Pastor Walter, what on earth are you doing here at this hour of the night?" I am sure she thought it had something to do with the church. Without giving me a chance to reply, she continued, "Come on in. Cham is in the living room."

I knew what my first words would be. Where our conversation would go from there, I had no idea. God had made it plain in His Word that a major part of my responsibility as a pastor is to *"...preach the Word: be instant in season, out of season: reprove, rebuke, encourage with all longsuffering and teaching."* He was also making it more clear all the time that this was to be done, not only from the pulpit to the whole congregation (that was easy), but to confront one on one as well (that was a bit more difficult).

My first words were a strong rebuke followed by a question. I opened with, "Minnie, earlier today Cham told me all about you and Del. Do you realize the horribleness of your sin?" She just sat there, stunned, and there were tears in Cham's eyes as he sat there on the couch beside her. "Cham even told me you want a divorce so you and Del can get married."

When she was able to speak, Minnie said, "Pastor, we are in love. I've never felt this way in my whole life. Del feels the same way, and he's going to ask his wife for a divorce, too."

After that statement, I could see that Cham was being torn apart down inside. "What about those vows you and Cham made before God, to love and cherish one another until death? Do you think He took you seriously when you made those vows before Him? Were YOU serious when you made them?" I asked.

Minnie never answered those questions, but her eyes began to well up with tears. I began again, "What about Sam, Shawn, and Debbie? What's going to happen to them?"

Minnie's answer to those questions I could not fathom. "I'm going to take them with me. Del is going to take his children with him, too, and we're going to raise them together", was her reply.

Out of total frustration with Minnie's answer to my questions, I responded with more questions. "Do you think Cham will allow an adulterous woman to raise his children while living with an adulterer husband who left his wife and children? What kind of a father do you think Cham is?"

Minnie's response, "I said Del wasn't going to leave his children. He is going to bring them along with us."

"When is all of this going to happen?" I asked.

"Not until Del can get things straightened around. It will be a while before he and his wife get their divorce."

"In the meantime, I suppose Del will come around when Cham is not home, to show you how much he loves you?" Then I addressed both Cham and Minnie, saying, "I guess the next thing for me to do is to go and talk to Del and his wife."

"No! No! Don't do that! Cham will lose his job!" Minnie exclaimed. My response: "Minnie, Cham is going to lose his job no matter what happens from here on. Only a fool would work for a man having an affair with his wife."

Let me give you some background that will help you to better understand what is happening. First of all, Del was Cham's boss, and the two were total opposites. Del was a man with an attractive personality, a salesman who gave the impression that he genuinely cared for others. His soft-spoken manner made people feel good about themselves (good qualities when they are genuine, and not misused on Minnie as he "sweet talked" her when they were alone).

Second, Cham was a typical hard-working, country man whose personality came across as a lot more coarse and crude than his boss, but he was real. I had known him for several years and saw him as a very caring man who was much better at expressing his care with deeds than with words (like the load of wood he had brought to me the evening before). I am sure he was the same way with his wife and family. He would do anything within his ability to please them, but there were few, if any, hugs and " I love you's."

Third, Del operated a small business with just a few men working for him, of which Cham was one. He always knew where Cham was during the day, and because he had two crews working, he traveled between them several times each day. This gave him the opportunities to see Minnie. His cover was to say that he was getting materials for one job or the other.

Fourth, Cham had told me that he had been suspicious for some time, thinking that there was something going on between Del and Minnie, and when he had confronted her about it, she had finally broken down and confessed to the whole affair and what her plans were (a divorce and a future with Del).

By now, Minnie was beginning to see the horrible consequences of her sinful affair with Del. She began to cry and blurted out, "I just wish this whole thing had never happened." Those were the first words she had spoken in the last two hours that gave me any hope, and they gave me the opportunity to tell her that her Heavenly Father was there to forgive her and welcome her back, just as the Father welcomed his wayward son home. (*LUKE 15:11-24*) All she had to do was come to Him in total repentance, as the prodigal son had done. He would forgive and restore her.

My next comment was, "I don't know about Cham, if he can forgive or not. Only he knows." Looking at Cham, I asked him, "What about it, Cham? Are Minnie and your family worth that much to you?"

Looking out through his teary, blood-shot eyes, his answer I will never forget. It was not the words so much as the tone in which he said them that was troubling. Then he continued, "I can forgive and will forgive. I'm not the perfect husband either, but if that b _ _ _ _ _ _ ever comes around here again, I'll not kill him, but I can assure you that he will need help getting back to his home."

I responded to his statement with words many might think un-Christian. I said, "Cham, you go to work tomorrow morning, take Del aside, tell him you quit, and tell him the same words you just told us."

He did just that, and Minnie remained faithful to him to the day he went home to be with the Lord, many, many years later, and Del never came around again either.

To my knowledge, no one ever knew about Cham's and Minnie's attack from Satan, upon their home, other than them, Del, my wife, and myself. I do not know if Del's wife ever knew. Maybe Del was making up the whole thing about getting a divorce.

The day I left that pastorate, Cham and Minnie came to the parsonage to wish us well. After a few minutes of expressing our love for each other, on the way out the door, Cham grabbed my hand, and pressing a twenty dollar bill into it, said these words, "Thank you Pastor, for everything. Thank you for saving our home."

Minnie added, "That goes for me, too."

In actuality, I did nothing but follow God's Instructions in *II TIMOTHY 2:24-26*. It was our *God of all grace that granted them repentance to the acknowledging of the truth that they were able to recover themselves out of the snare of the devil.* God does His work inside people. We only see the outward results, and only my wife and I saw those outward results in Cham's and Minnie's lives. Again, no one else even knew anything had happened. Thank the Lord. As a Co-Worker with God I have seen Him fix many things few people ever knew were broken.

Spirit Enlightened, Spirit Taught + Faith = <u>CHANGED LIVES</u>

Mr. V and Mrs. F

Through the years I have come to know a number of those who had come to know Jesus Christ and continued to grow and mature in Him without the benefit of a Bible believing, teaching church. They all had two things in common. They believed that the Bible was Gods Word, and **they *also* read and studied it**. The Holy Spirit was their teacher. He had imparted, to each, a God given faith that comes from hearing His Word (*ROM: 10:17*)

Many years ago, as I was visiting with one old fellow who fit the above description, he said, "I hear they are rewriting the Bible. I don't think the Bible needs to be rewritten. It just needs to be reread and believed."

He had a point. His evident faith in Christ, his well-worn Bible, and his godly life were testimony to what the Holy Spirit does in one who reads and rereads and believes God's Word. The following are accounts of two just like him.

Mr. V

It is evident that God is working in a person when that person wants everyone to know the Lord, not get them merely to "come to church." Floyd, a man I mentioned in my previous book, the man who was a trapper, who worked with me day after day to rebuild the parsonage at the T. B. C. church, was a prime example of such a person. I have not known many of this type of Christian, even though we all know we should be.

In those early years of his relationship with Christ, he was talking to everyone about Christ: his sister and brother in law, his hunting buddies, his buddies at work, the town policeman, and on and on. After many of those witnessing encounters, Floyd would come to me and say, "Pastor, I need you again. Will you go along with me and help me explain what it means to *know the Lord?* They think I'm just trying to convert them to my religion." (Years later, when I taught the psychology course, at what is now Davis College, I explained to each class the fact that when we speak of God and Jesus Christ, most people don't hear what we are saying. They hear the word *religion* instead of *God*. Unless the Holy Spirit, through His Word, enlightens their understanding, *religion* is all they hear.)

On one of those occasions, Floyd wanted me to go along to talk to a man he described using words like kind, caring, loving, and good. He said this man was like a father to him as he was growing up. Floyd wanted to find out if he was a Biblical Christian or just a good man. We arrived at Mr. V's home at 7:00 P.M. and left after midnight. What a great evening!

As we knocked on Mr. V's door, I could see Floyd was nervous. What were we about to find out? Floyd and I were carrying our Bibles. Mr. V noticed this immediately and with a smile, gave us a cheery, "Come on in."

Floyd introduced me to Mr. V and we took our seats on an old couch while Mr. V sat in a rocking chair. By his side was an old stand with a Bible on top of several other books. After several minutes of preliminaries, mostly Floyd and Mr. V reminiscing, with a few questions from Mr. V directed to me, it was my turn to do the questioning. "Mr. V, I'm going to tell you why we are here this evening. Since Floyd became a Christian, he wants to take me to all of his friends to tell them about Christ. You are one of those friends he says he has known all of his life. He has told me some things about you and thinks highly of you. He says you are one of the friendliest, kind, and caring people he has ever known. What he wants to know is if you are a Christian or just a good man?"

The smile on Mr. V's face told the answer before he verbally answered the question. "Yes, Floyd, I'm a Christian, but I'm not sure I'm quite as nice a man as you have me painted in your mind," he said with a laugh.

My next question was, "Mr. V, what is a Christian?"

Pointing to a plaque on the wall, he replied, "See that picture, (it was a picture of Christ knocking at a door), a Christian is one who has heard Christ's voice asking for entrance. I heard His voice and let Him in more than fifty years ago." Pointing to his breast he continued, "He still lives here. He has promised He will never leave me nor forsake me."

With those words, he reached over and picked up his well-worn Bible. As he opened it, he said, "I see you fellows have Bibles, too. I have some questions I would like to ask you."

The discussion that followed those words lasted for the next five hours and would have lasted all night if I had not promised my wife I would be home by midnight (I did tell her a "little" lie, for it was nearer 1:00 A.M. when we did get home).

There is neither space nor time to go into all the subjects we talked about that night as we turned from one passage to another in God's Word. I have never before, or since, seen one of God's children enjoying a five hour Bible discussion more than Mr. V did that night, and the one other conversation I had with him, in the hospital just before he died, some years later. Those two instances left such an impression on me that I have used them as illustrations in sermons many times over the forty-five years since they took place.

Of all the subjects we talked about that night, the return of Christ was number one. We turned from one passage to another, reading prophecy after prophecy and promise after promise. We talked about how He changed our lives when He came in to live and how He continued to change us as we spent time in His Word. Finally, and best of all, we discussed how we would be like Him when we saw Him *face to face*.

We looked back to the Cross on which He died for our sins and on back to the event called "the Fall" in *GENESIS 3* that brought about the need for the Cross. We went back farther to *GENESIS 1 and 2* and looked at what God's original creation was like, and how we (mankind) were created in His Image and Likeness, and then even further back through the pages of God's Revelation to see that all of this was a part of God's eternal purpose, that the Lamb that is to come and the Lamb that gave His life for our sins at Calvary, was *the Lamb slain before the foundation of the world.*

We talked about heaven and what it will be like. Flipping the pages of our Bibles from one passage to another, we were not aware of all God was doing in each of us that night, but there was to be one more meeting with Mr. V sometime later, that would reveal that God had cemented a bond between the three of us that we all knew was an eternal bond. We were one in Christ, and we all knew it.

Before giving an account of that second and last meeting, I must tell what transpired as we got up after five hours of being seated on that couch and rocking chair. Mr. V put his hand on the door knob and said, "Before you fellows leave, I must say something. It has been many years since I have been able to talk to a pastor about the things we've discussed this evening. The pastors we have had in our church down here in recent years didn't preach much from the Bible. They talk more about current social and political issues. I can't begin to tell you how much I have enjoyed this evening. I won't soon forget it." After these words, we all bowed our heads and prayed together.

What a time of rejoicing Floyd and I had on the way home! Floyd's question was answered. Mr. V was not only a good, moral man, but a brother in Christ, who loved God and His Word every bit as much as we did.

That was the first and last meeting I had with Mr. V until I received a telephone call from a hospital some years later. They said they had a patient who said he would like to see me. His name was Mr. V. I drove to that hospital that very day. Upon entering his room, his first words, in a much weaker tone than that night several years before, were, "Pastor Walter, I'm so glad you could come. I wanted to see you again before I go home. I'm not talking about my home up there in the country. I'll probably never get back up there. I'm talking about going home to be with our Lord."

For the next forty-five minutes, there in that small hospital room, two redeemed men were speaking of their Redeemer Who had gone on before, to prepare a place in *the Father's House* to be their eternal home (*JOHN 14:1-3*). They quoted Scripture after Scripture that spoke of the *Cross* and how "The Way of the Cross Leads Home." They spoke of death, not as that horrible thing brought upon all mankind by the sin in the **third chapter** in their Bibles, but as that enemy that had been conquered and defeated by their crucified, risen, and ascended Lord. They spoke of themselves as two strangers and pilgrims, who, like Pilgrim of "Pilgrims Progress," *looked for a city with foundations who's Builder and Maker was God*. They both knew that in the very near future, one of them would be there, and they both knew this hope was theirs solely and wholly by the grace of God.

Those forty-five minutes in that hospital room were simply the continuation and culmination of the Bible discussion we had had that evening some years before. Discussion did I say? It was far more than that! Theologically speaking, it was what the ancient creed called "Communion of saints." I am sure it will continue along with that great cloud of witnesses and all those strangers and pilgrims that have followed after, when we all get home (*HEBREWS 11 and 12*).

Mr. V is one example of a great TRUTH, and that is, that God transforms lives by His Holy Spirit, through the written Word, sometimes without a Bible teaching church and pastor.

He had come to know Christ at an early age by reading God's Word, and continued to grow through his personal reading and study of God's Word. His well-worn Bible was an added evidence of his faith and obedience to his Redeemer and Lord. His words to me as I walked into that hospital room, shortly before he died, were the final evidence of a God transformed heart. He was **anxiously** looking forward to going home to be with his Lord.

Mrs. F

Let me tell you of another like Mr. V. She was my daughter's music teacher more than forty years ago. Like Mr. V, she had little help in understanding God's Word, from the church she occasionally attended.

She was an elderly widow when I first met her. My first thought at that time was, "What a sweet old lady." She lived alone in a small town, eight miles from where we lived. One hour a week for several years we took our daughter to her home for piano lessons. Sometimes we (my wife and/or I) waited outside in our car for that hour, but in bad weather we went inside during her lesson. I can still hear Mrs. F's welcome to me, to help myself to any of the books that were on her book shelves. What a treat! She had no idea how I loved to read. I was never ready to leave when our daughter's lesson was done. If Mrs. F didn't have another student immediately following, we often talked for a few minutes. More often than not, our conversations started with me mentioning something I had read in one of her books.

One such time I remember well was the time I had read George Washington's farewell address. When I quoted the line from that famous address: "Beware of any philosophy that would teach morality can be maintained apart from religion (Christianity)," we entered into a lengthy discussion about religion and present day morality. I soon found that Mrs. F's views on the Bible, its Christ, and morality were the same as mine. From that evening on, I knew we shared a much closer relationship than just a parent and our daughter's piano teacher. We shared many good times together during the next year, after our daughter's piano lessons. We had many discussions of a spiritual nature and several intimate discussions where she shared things about her past and her family that I am sure she had never mentioned to anyone for years. They were all things that were of a spiritual nature that left her with unanswered questions. Using the Bible, I tried to explain what God had to say about her unanswered questions.

Then, there came a very sad evening for all of us (my daughter, my wife, and me). Mrs. F informed us that she had a terminal disease and would no longer be teaching piano lessons.

Over the months that followed, we visited Mrs. F several times. It was evident, at each successive visit, that she was getting weaker. Soon she would have to go to a nursing home. She said her neighbors, who had been looking after her many times each day, could not take care of all that needed to be done, because she needed around the clock care.

We felt so sorry for her, because we knew how much she hated the thought of going into a nursing home. I tried to comfort her by telling her what a nice place this particular nursing home was. Her response was, "Pastor Walter, I know it is a good nursing home, but you just don't understand."

She was right, and I would not understand until several weeks after her death. When I did find out what she meant by those words, I cried. Read on, and if this does not bring tears to your eyes, I will be surprised.

Nearly two months had passed since Mrs. F had entered the nursing home. I had visited her several times and found her weaker each time. Then, one evening, as we were eating supper, I received a telephone call from the nursing home, informing me that Mrs. F wanted to see me. The nurse who called said Mrs. F was very weak.

Upon entering Mrs. F's room, speaking slowly and with a very weak voice, she said, "Pastor Walter, thank you for coming. There are two things I want you to do for me. Will you read the *23rd Psalm* to me and then pray that I die tonight?"

I was taken aback by that last request and responded by saying, "I'll gladly read the *23rd Psalm* and pray for you, but I cannot pray that you will die tonight."

With her voice now getting weaker and weaker, she pleaded, "Please, please, If I don't die soon there will be a lot of disappointed people that I love. I know you don't understand, but you will."

She was right, I did not understand. Nevertheless, I read the *23rd Psalm* and then remarked, "The *23rd Psalm* is the middle of three Psalms that form a Trilogy. The *22nd Psalm* is "**Christ the Good Shepherd dying for His Sheep**. The *23rd Psalm* is "**Christ the Great Shepherd *Caring for His Sheep***. The *24th Psalm* is "**Christ the Chief Shepherd, the King of Glory,**" *Coming to Reign with His Sheep.*"

With that remark, her whole demeanor changed, and she asked this question, "Before you leave, can you teach that outline to me?"

The next hour with Mrs. F was a blessed but strenuous time. The lesson I was about to teach, I had taught and preached before, both to a class and to a congregation from the pulpit, but this was different. Now I had a congregation of one; an ill, elderly, dying lady whose body was totally worn out and a mind that had slowed to a crawl.

Two aspects about my **congregation of one** completely outweighed the negatives. Although Mrs. F.'s mental faculties had slowed tremendously from the days when she was teaching our daughter, just over a year before, they were still intact. More importantly, here was one of God's Children who *wanted* to "grow in grace and knowledge of her Heavenly Shepherd." He had said, while here on earth, *"Blessed are* they which do hunger and thirst after righteousness, *for they shall be filled."*

I began by reading the *22ⁿᵈ Psalm* which is a vivid description of death by crucifixion, written more than six hundred years before it was even invented by the Romans.

Then I read the *24ᵗʰ Psalm* which speaks of the "Coming of the King of Glory *(The Chief Shepherd)*. Now comes the memorizing of the titles of the three Psalms mentioned above. I have never before or since seen someone more determined to learn. Just like she was with her music students, now she was with herself. Time after time she would say to them and now to me, "Now, let's go over that again." She would not give up until she had it down pat in her *memory,* or should I say her *heart?* After a good hour, she could say them without any prompting on my part.

PSALM 22 – "Christ the Good Shepherd Dying for His Sheep"
PSALM 23 – "Christ the Great Shepherd Caring for His Sheep"
PSALM 24 – "Christ the Chief Shepherd, the King of Glory, Coming to Reign with His Sheep"

I said, "Let us pray before I go."

Then came that request from her again, with a little variation in the wording. She said, "Please, and don't forget to pray that I die soon."

I did pray, and simply closed my prayer, saying, "May Your will be done in Mrs. F's life."

Early the next morning the telephone rang. A person at the nursing home said, "Pastor Walter, Mrs. F passed away during the night."

I wasn't surprised, but how would I ever know what she had meant when she had said, "If I don't die soon, a lot of people (my friends) will be disappointed?"

My answer came in the mail several weeks later, in a large, thick envelope. It was from a law firm and contained Mrs. F's will. Page after page, and over and over again I read, "*In appreciation for...*" "**In appreciation** for all those times they checked to see if I was all right or needed anything, I bequeath to Bob and Betty, my neighbors, the sum of $5,000. Those words, **"In appreciation..."** preceded dozens of statements and peoples' names. Everyone who had helped Mrs. F, from the boy who shoveled her sidewalk to her next door neighbors, she left sums of money ranging from $100 to $5,000 each.

Reading down through that list, near the end was my name. That statement read, "**In appreciation** for the two shrubs he planted in front of my home, I bequeath to Rev. James Walter, the sum of $100."

That was something I had totally forgotten about until I read those words. One day, when I had taken my daughter to her piano lesson, I had two yews left over from a landscaping job I had done. I had them in the back of my station wagon, and while my daughter was taking her lesson, I planted them, one on each side of her porch steps. At that time, she wanted to pay me for them, but I told her there wasn't any charge; they were a gift.

Now I knew why Mrs. F wanted to die. She knew her money would soon be gone if she lingered on in that nursing home. She couldn't bear the thought of having her will read and no money left for all those to whom she wished to show her gratitude, not in words only, but in a tangible way, after her death.

Mrs. F like Mr. V wasn't in a local church that faithfully taught the Word of God, but God, through His Word, which they believed, had transformed their lives.

God, by His Spirit, through His Word, changes people. What a privilege it is to be His co-laborer and be allowed to witness one of His own growing in the grace and knowledge of Him, nearly up to the moment she left her body to go to be with Him.

GOD'S UNDER-SHEPHERDS:
God's Co-Laborers
Their Calling, Their Work

"They watch for your souls as they that must give account."
HEBREWS 13:17

"Take heed therefore unto yourselves, and all the flock over the which the Holy Spirit has made you overseers, to feed the church of God, which He has purchased with His own blood, for I know this, that after my departing shall grievous wolves enter in among you, not sparing the flock. Also, of your own selves shall men arise, speaking perverse things, to draw away disciples after them." ACTS 20:28-30

"Do you love me more than these?' ***"Yes Lord"***

"Then feed MY lambs...Feed MY sheep...Tend MY sheep."
JOHN 21:16, 17

F.B. Meyer, in his book, "Tried by Fire," wrote, "It is not enough to preach to the flock once or twice each week. There must be personal supervision. *There must be watching for souls as by those who must give account,* seeking them if they go astray, tracking them to the precipice down which they have fallen; and never resting 'til the straying sheep is brought again to the fold. All this is included in the Word and we need to do all this if we are to *tend* THE FLOCK OF GOD."

SECTION TWO

God Through his Word Delivering From
Sins
Addictions
Offenses
Roots of Bitterness

C all them by whatever name you wish, they are all contrary to
the nature of the God of the Bible. They are not a complete
list by any means (sins, addictions, offenses, roots of bitterness).
There could be added "false teachings," or using some of the secular
world's terms that include all of the "manias" and "phobias" with
their prefixes.

Just what are we talking about anyway? We are talking about
all the incidents found, even in the lives of those who profess to be
God's Children, through faith in Jesus Christ, that are inspired by
Satan. We are talking about all of those incidents that are recorded in
the Old and the New Testaments that caused divisions and disunity
in the family and the Church and disgrace to the Eternal God Who
ordained both. We are talking about the lies and deceit in the families of Abraham, Isaac, and Jacob. We are talking about the immoral
acts of men like Judah, Samson, and David. We are talking about
the jealousies and envies such as we saw in the family of Aaron,
Miriam, and Moses. We are talking about the lust and idolatry manifested in the lives of the children of Israel while on their way from

Egypt to Canaan. We are talking about the "holier than thou" attitudes of most religious leaders at the time of our Lord's sojourn here. We are talking about the greedy Ananiases and Saphiras of the early Church at Jerusalem. We are talking about the Euodias and Syntyches who are at odds with each other, causing divisions in the church. We are talking about those who were committing fornication, were covetous, gossipers, etc., in the church at Corinth. We are talking about the Hymenaeuses and Alexanders who brought false doctrines into the Church. We are talking about the Diotrephes' who must have the preeminence in the Church or they are miffed. Then there are all those tempers, like Moses, the meekest man in all the earth who, on two occasions, displayed his with dire consequences, and let us not forget Peter's temper (temperament) along with his boastful attitude before Pentecost. He even cursed and denied his Lord! Three times!! (*LUKE 22:31-34*).

Do these things still happen in families and local churches today? To get a bit more personal, do any of them find their way into your life and mine?

Before we look into another attack of the Evil One, let me give you a list of statements any pastor hears only too often. Many of them, if not confronted immediately by a humble, loving, caring brother, will end up in a fractured home, and many times, in divorce or a disunited church family. Blessed is the local church that has **a pastor with a father's heart instead of a judge's heart**, to use the Word of God to confront each situation **ONE ON ONE**, as it arises. Doubly blessed is the local church that has **those living and walking in the Spirit, whose hearts are broken when a brother or sister is "...*overtaken in a fault...*" (sin) (GALATIANS 6:1, 2).**

In Christ there is *forgiveness* and *reconciliation* for the *repentant* sinner and in Christ there is *forgiveness, cleansing, deliverance,* and *restoration* for the *repentant* brother.

In most, but not every situation represented by the following list of statements and illustrations, God saw fit to transform lives by His forgiveness, cleansing, deliverance, and restoration.

"*The Word of God is living and powerful*" and when accompanied by His Holy Spirit, *changes lives.* **I can assure you, a humble, meek, Spirit filled person using the Word of God, is**

going to see more changed lives than any educated counselor who relies on his knowledge, education, and skill.

THE UGLY LIST

1. "My husband (wife) is having an affair with another person."
2. "Our daughter is having an affair with J.N."
3. From a fearful, guilt-ridden wife and mother, "Marjorie (one of her children) doesn't belong to my husband, but he doesn't know it. I had an affair with his best friend when he was away on a business trip. Many times over the last seven years he has said he can't figure out when Marjorie was conceived. What should I do? I can't take this guilt much longer. Every time I look into Marjorie's eyes I can see J.," (her husband's best friend).
4. "My oldest daughter's father is not my husband. Her father is Pastor S.'s. brother. He and I had an affair one summer when he was visiting Pastor S. and his family.
5. "My dad is trying to do bad things to me, and when I told Mom about it, she wouldn't believe me."
6. "My dad raped me when I was thirteen," (at the time her dad was a deacon in the church).
7. "I am in a lesbian relationship with P. I want to quit doing these things we are doing with each other, but when we are together alone they just seem to happen."
8. "Someone ought to warn Norris. The girl he is engaged to marry is a lesbian."
9. "I had an abortion, and I feel awful about it most of the time."
10. "My husband is all mixed up in pornography. He wants me to look at this rotten stuff and then do it with him and others he invites over." She then handed me five of the filthiest booklets of photographs of every conceivable sex act any deranged mind could imagine.
11. "My husband is up all hours of the night chatting with women on the internet. I can't take it much longer."
12 "My husband is so jealous and fearful that I am going to cheat on him that he calls me at least six to eight times a day to make sure I'm home. His fears and jealousy scares me."

13. "My husband doesn't allow enough money in the family budget to live on. All he thinks about is 'himself and his play things.'"
14. "Our family is totally divided over our mom's death. It's about the inheritance. Greed, greed, greed!" (A common occurrence)
15. "Our son (a teenager) has been caught shoplifting again. We don't know which way to turn."
16. "Our daughter has admitted to having affairs with two married men. Now she says she's a lesbian. We're devastated."
17. "My wife (husband) gets mad at me and sometimes doesn't speak to me for days at a time. Can you help us?" (Another common occurrence)
18. "I'm afraid of my husband. When he gets angry, he's out of control."
19. "My husband has been accused of exposing himself."
20. "If those new people don't like the way we do things here, let them go somewhere else."
21. "Who do those new people think they are? They come in here and just think they can take over."
22. Said to a young couple the second Sunday they came to our Young Couples Class: "You're too old for this class. You'll have to go in with the older class."
23. Again, about *new people:* "They think they're too good for us, just because they've got money. We do not need them around here anyway".
24. Spoken by a mother to her two young children: "Pastor Walter doesn't teach the Truth anymore, so we are going to go to another church," (told to me by the Sunday school teacher of one of those two children).
25. Spoken by a man destroying an adult Sunday school class with his argumentative attitude: "Mr. B. (the Sunday school class teacher) has been teaching lies, and now the pastor is, too."
26. From a very sincere person who was deceived by false teaching and was trying to convince others to leave the church and go with them where the Truth was taught: "Pastor, you have time to see this, my sister and brother in law have time to see this, and my mother has time to see this, but the thing that bothers

me most, is that I have a dad in hell tonight (with tears running down his cheeks). For him it is forever too late."

27. Said by a leader in the church: "Pastor, they might be saved, but they're trouble. We're better off without them."

28. Told to me about several leaders in the church: "They got rid of the last pastor, and when they get tired of you, they'll do the same with you."

29. "I'm not in with that clique, nor do I want to be."

30. From a deacon whom I had asked to go with me to talk to his neighbor: "I'm not going to talk to him. He did me dirt years ago. I want nothing to do with him,"

31. 1:00 A.M. "Pastor please come quick" (A domestic fight again).

32. From a concerned parent:. "Pastor, Mrs.C (their children's Music teacher) is turning my children against their Youth Leader by criticizing him week after week. They don't want to go to their youth meetings any more. I thought you ought to know this is happening."

33. From the police: "Rev. Walter, we are quite sure the one who broke into your home and stole that money is a boy in your church." (Dannie) Note—You will read about Dannie later on in this book.

The list goes on and on, each one either from or about those who claim to be children of God, through faith in Jesus Christ.

Right here I am going to reveal the heart of an under-shepherd and co-laborer with God. Upon hearing of, or seeing any of the above situations, his heart (the under-shepherd's) aches and breaks. He knows what he must do, because he hears the Holy Spirit say, *"Brethren, if a man be overtaken in a fault, ye who are spiritual restore such an one IN THE SPIRIT OF MEEKNESS, considering thyself, lest thou also be tempted," (GALATIANS 6:1).*

*"The servant of the Lord **must not strive**, but be gentle unto all men, apt to teach, **PATIENT.** IN MEEKNESS instructing them that oppose themselves, if GOD, PERADVENTURE, WILL GIVE THEM REPENTANCE TO THE ACKNOWLEDGING OF THE TRUTH, and that they may recover themselves out of the snare of the devil, who are taken captive by him at his will," (II TIMOTHY 2:24-26).*

*"I charge thee therefore, before God, and the Lord Jesus Christ, who shall judge the living and the dead at His appearing and His kingdom: Preach the Word; be instant in season, out of season; reprove, rebuke, encourage **WITH ALL LONG-SUFFERING** and doctrine (teaching),"* (II TIMOTHY 4:1, 2).

"Now we exhort you brethren, WARN_the unruly, COMFORT the feebleminded, SUPPORT *the weak,* **BE PATIENT TOWARD ALL**,*"* (I THESSALONIANS 5:14). The apostle Paul, who penned these instructions, also, by his example, instructed God's co-laborers where and when they were to be implemented. To the elders at the church at Ephesus, he said, *"I kept back nothing that was profitable unto you but HAVE SHOWED YOU and have taught you PUBLICLY, and from HOUSE TO HOUSE,"* (ACTS 20:20).

Preaching publicly against sins, addictions, offenses, and roots of bitterness will, for the most part, get a pastor **pats on the back**. Being a Nathan and going to the guilty David individually and saying to his face *"**Thou art the man**"* is another story. Confrontations are not fun, and often, at least in the beginning, filled with a lot of anger and defensive response, but any co-laborer together with God, knows that if he goes in love and with concern for the offender's good and God's Glory, trusting God to honor His Word, there will be victory after victory (not always immediately, for God's Co-Workers *"... **MUST BE PATIENT**..."* (II TIMOTHY 2:24).

"Unity and Harmony" maintained without violating God's Truth is almost a full-time job for any pastor (shepherd) in any local church body today. The Evil One; that "Old Deceiver," "Divider," and "Destroyer," the Heavenly Shepherd's Arch Enemy, is ever active, sowing seeds of discord among God's people. He knows that unity is that which makes a local church a living testimony for God's Glory and a shining light in the surrounding community.

It is not the message preached week after week within the walls of a building, nor is it the strong doctrinal statements written on paper, to which we all give assent, nor is it the manner in which a local body conducts their worship services (as important as all of these things may be), that makes a church a testimony in the community where it is located. It is not the hundreds (maybe even thousands) of Bible verses we have memorized and crammed away in our minds, nor is it those fifteen minute devotions we have each morning. It is not the sinful things that we are against, and for the most part, do not do ourselves. It is not even our outward, verbal profession of faith in Jesus Christ.

Then, what is it that makes a local church a testimony for the Lord? It is a family of God's *obedient children,* saved by grace, through faith, walking in the good works God has before ordained (*EPHESIANS 2:8-10*). It is also God's children walking worthy of their calling *"with all lowliness and meekness, with long-suffering, for-bearing one another in love," (EPHESIANS 4:1, 2).* It is God's children imitating the Heavenly Father by putting away the self-centered filth of the world and walking in love and light (*EPHESIANS 5:1-8).* It is a beautiful cluster of "the fruit of the Spirit (*love, joy, peace, long-suffering, gentleness, goodness, meekness, faithful-ness, self-control*) hanging from the Heavenly Vine, for all to see (*JOHN 15:1-14; 13:33-35; GALATIANS 5:22-23).* It is His children in whom He is working *"...both to will and to do of His good plea-sure, doing all things without murmurings and disputings, shining as lights in this dark world,"* in which we live, *"Holding forth the word of life..." (Philippians 2:12-16).*

In summary, it is God's little children, ***not merely believing Truth,*** but His children ***walking in Truth*** and obeying His two New Testament commandments: ***Believe in Jesus Christ and Love one another*** *(II JOHN 4; I JOHN 3:18, 23-24; 4:7-8, 11-12).*

The apostle John was expressing his Heavenly Father's heart, and as well, the heart of any of His faithful under-shepherds, when he wrote, *"I have no greater joy than to hear that my (God's) chil-dren WALK IN TRUTH.(III JOHN 4).*

These things glorify our Heavenly Father and make a local body a testimony for Him (*MATTHEW 5:16*), but, oh *"... the little foxes, that spoil the vine; for our vines have tender grapes," (SONG of SOLOMON 2:15).*

The worst of those little foxes is the little member in all our mouths called the tongue, for, *"The tongue is a fire, a world of iniq-uity..." (James 3:6).* When we use it to express our old Adamic nature it hurts, divides, angers, spreads and destroys, and most times, its fallout victims are the innocent. Putting back together the broken relationships caused by the tongue, is many times more difficult than putting Humpty Dumpty back together again. "All the king's horses and all the king's men" could not do that, and only the power of God's Word, spoken in love can restore relationships broken by an uncontrolled tongue.

God's Word says that the last enemy to be destroyed is death (*I CORINTHIANS 15:26),* and I believe that the last member of our bodies, to be controlled is "the tongue."

An Offense of The Tongue

The Dutch Door

"Who do these new people think they are? They come in here and just think they can take over."

Those words were spoken outside an overcrowded church nursery, after a Sunday morning Worship service. The repercussions from those words reverberated for months. *"Behold, how great a matter a little fire kindleth!" (JAMES 3:5).*

Please allow me to digress for a moment. I remember when there were no nurseries in most country churches. Families sat together during the Sunday Worship service, from the oldest to the youngest (including infants). There were few services without one or two crying babies. If the bottle, or today, the "binkie," did not stop the crying, the mother simply took the baby out of the service until it stopped crying. Back at that time, that was what was expected, and for the most part, accepted, as a normal part of the Sunday Worship Service. Most old-time pastors were of the mindset that crying babies were no problem, and as the babies got louder and louder, so did he.

I'm sure many have heard the story of the mother who got up to carry her crying baby outside and the pastor said, "You don't have to take your baby outside, he's not bothering me."

Her response as she went out the door was, "That's not the problem. You're bothering him."

Well, things are different today. All churches have nurseries, and all of those annoying, crying babies are in those nurseries. Mothers are now free to enjoy the services and meetings of the church. Nearly everywhere you go today, you will see the words "Nursery provided."

Don't get me wrong, I am for nurseries being provided for church services, although, I do sometimes wonder if the Church is not unwittingly contributing to the weakening of the family unit by providing everything for every age group from nursery to senior citizens' centers. It seems that churches provide few times where the whole family is together. We even divide up our worship services, but that's better left for another chapter. Here and now we are talking about a fire that started outside a church nursery, ignited by those words quoted at the beginning of this chapter.

Here is the setting. Our church family was in the midst of a baby boom. Our small nursery had to be enlarged, so we had cribs stacked two high. Even so, there still was not enough room on Sundays when all of the babies were there.

The church had elected two mothers to be the "nursery directors." It was their job to oversee the nursery, and at that time, there were twelve to seventeen babies in there during the Sunday morning services. These two mothers soon learned that this was more than a two man (woman) job. They believed that some changes were necessary, and in fact, had a list of those changes in hand. They had already contacted several of the mothers who were quite enthusiastic about the proposed changes. I read over the list, and everything sounded good, except the last one. **"No one shall be permitted in the nursery except those appointed to be in charge of the nursery for a given service, The only exception being the mothers, and then, only if a mother is needed for some reason."**

They explained to me, the pandemonium that ensued after a Sunday morning service, when, literally, dozens of people packed into that small nursery (mothers, of course, brothers and sisters of babies, and then, a half-dozen or so GRANDMAS). Their idea was that even the mothers did not need to enter the nursery to drop off their babies or to pick them up. They could be dropped off at the nursery door and picked up at the door after the service. Then they told me that the mothers they had contacted liked the idea.

I jokingly asked, "How do you propose to keep people out, have a policeman guard the door?"

They laughed and told me they had that problem all figured out. What they needed was a "Dutch door" with a wide ledge on the top of the bottom section so the babies and their diaper bags could be handed in over that ledge. Their explanation was, "That way, we can lock the bottom door from the inside and just open the top door so we can hand the babies and their bags, over that ledge, to their mothers after the service." Then they asked, "Where can we get a Dutch door?"

I answered that question by saying, "No problem. You will have your Dutch door by Sunday, and it will cost no one a penny."

The only materials needed to turn that nursery door into a Dutch door were a wide piece of five-quarter stock, another pair of hinges, , and a barrel bolt to hold the two door sections together when they either wanted both halves of the door open or closed at the same time, and I knew where to find all of those things. Three hours later the new nursery directors had their Dutch door, and with it, something else coming Sunday morning that no one had foreseen. What could possibly happen?

Several GRANDMAS who were used to rushing from the Sunday Worship service to the nursery to see their darling, little grandbabies, found the bottom part of the new Dutch door closed, and "locked" from the inside. When they were told they could not go in, as we Dutchmen would say, **"The fur flew"**.

Those sweet, loving, now IRATE GRANDMAS gathered around the door and wanted to know whose idea this was, and when they were told it was the idea of the **new nursery directors**, one of them spoke out, loudly and clearly enough for them and all passersby to hear, **"Who do these new people think they are? They come in here and just think they can take over!"**

At the time, they did not know that I had made the Dutch door. If they had known that, they probably would not have shaken my hand as they left the auditorium, on their way to the nursery, just fifteen or twenty feet away (Ha Ha). I do know that when I went to their homes that next week, to try to put out the fires started by those words, they weren't very happy with me, and you know, they still felt that same way toward those new nursery directors. In their minds, those nursery directors were still **intruders from the outside** and not "**co-laborers together with God**" in building His Church.

There was no way they were going to apologize for their nasty remark. They did not seem to mind the pandemonium in the nursery Sunday after Sunday after every morning service. To them, it was just their time to see and hug their "darling, little grandbabies," and it did not matter that the nursery had become a zoo. In fact, the words of a young fellow with a great sense of humor described how he looked at the nursery with the new Dutch door, saying, "Hey fellows, look! The zoo is closed to the public! Only the zookeepers and their helpers are allowed in to watch all of those cute, little monkeys in their cages!" They laughed and moved on.

No one was offended by those words. Actually, having a sense of humor myself, I could see their point, with that little room and all of those cribs and their bars, stacked on top of each other on three walls, and how many parents, after watching their child do some new, cute thing, have said, "Why, you little monkey?" I know I have.

I had several sessions with the nursery directors over that incident, and they assured me they, "had broad shoulders," and could handle those nasty words. Of course that sounded great to me, except, the way they handled them was to tell one after another what those **mean-spirited grandmothers** had said about them. The Old Divider was working, and tongues were wagging. The issue was, not so much the nursery door, but those words, "**new people.**" They clearly revealed that this church, to operate as a body, had a long way to go.

Every time I hear the words "**New People, Senior Saints, or Them and Us,**" I know there is disunity within that local church. They will never be used by anyone who sees the local church as a family of God's children. There may be babies, the immature, and the weak, but everyone who knows he is a child in God's family, knows he is so by *grace alone,* and is no better than any other brother or sister in the family of God. Today, so many churches are merely religious organizations people join and attend until someone or something (usually a loose tongue) crosses them, and off they go to another local church. Is it any wonder an unbelieving world is so often tuned out when we try to tell them about our wonderful Lord? He, Himself said, *"A new commandment I give unto you, that ye love one another; as I have loved you, that ye also love one another," (JOHN 13:34, 35)*.

Incidentally, those two families left the church within the next two years. When I asked them their reason for leaving "**their church family**," the first thing mentioned was the Dutch door incident. "We never felt we were a part of **this church family** since the day that incident took place.

Unity in a church family sounds like such a simple matter. All that is needed is a group of God's believing children practicing God's *"ONE ANOTHERS"* He gave to His Church throughout the New Testament. Violating these seems to be **no big deal** to so many of us who claim to believe and stand for the *"...whole counsel of God."* Are not these *"ONE ANOTHERS"* a part of that counsel? Here is a partial list of them:

1. *"...love one another..." I JOHN 3:23-24; JOHN 13:35*
2. *"...pray for one another..." JAMES 5:16*
3. *"...care one for another..." I CORINTHIANS 12:25*
4. *"...serve one another." GALATIANS 5:13*
5. *"Bear one another's burdens..." GALATIANS 6:2s*
6. *"Forbearing (being patient with) one another..." COLOSSIANS 3:13*
7. *"And be ye kind one to another, tenderhearted toward one another..." EPHESIANS 4:32*
8. *"...forgive one another..." COLOSSIANS 3:13; EPHESIANS 4:32*
9. *"Submitting yourselves one to another..." EPHESIANS 5:21*
10. *"Wherefore, comfort one another..." I THESSALONIANS 4:18*
11. *"Exhort (encourage) one another..." HEBREWS 3:13*
12. *"...have compassion one of another..." I PETER 3:8*
13. *"...be subject one to another..." I PETER 5:5*

14. *"Do not bite and devour one another..."* GALATIANS 5:15
15. *"Do not envy one another..."* GALATIANS 5:26
16. *"Lie not one to another..."* COLOSSIANS 3:4
17. *"Judge not one another..."* ROMANS 14:13

We close this list with the one with which we began, *"LOVE ONE ANOTHER."* If we practiced this **"one"** we would automatically practice the other sixteen. That is what the **Book of First John** is all about.

Jealousy, Anger, and Bitterness

Whoa! Hold it right there!" Those were the words spoken to me by a high school guidance counselor many, many years ago. They were words of rebuke as I was in the midst of rebuking him.

A senior high girl from our church had shown me a book from the public school library, about **expressing our emotions**. The further I read, the more angry I became. I got so upset that I felt it was my duty as a pastor to go over to the school and let them know how I felt about many of the things that book contained. I knew the guidance counselor. He was my neighbor, living just up the street from the church.

I went directly to his office which was right next to the school library; with several quotes from the book that girl from the church had given to me. Two of those quotes follow, as nearly as I can recall them: **"We must give our children room to express their emotions. That means all emotions, including anger and even sexual feelings. If we stifle these emotions they will grow up not understanding how to vent these emotions all of us have. Not allowing them to express their emotions will only cause anger and hate to build, and when they grow up they will not be able to express their emotions in a constructive way."**

Second Quote **"As long as we are in a society that frowns upon sexual relations outside of marriage, we must teach our children ways to vent those sexual desires. I would suggest close dancing and light petting."** (The first part of the second quote certainly dates that book, doesn't it?)

89

As I handed him that book, pointing out those quotes, I made a major mistake. It was at the undeserved rebuke that he stopped me from finishing.

I had said, "You secular psychologists that teach…"

That's as far as I got before Mr. S. interrupted me with a rebuke of his own. Speaking calmly but firmly he said, "Whoa! Hold it right there! I resent your classifying me in with all psychologists. How would you like it if I classified you in with all preachers? First of all, I want you to know that I am in agreement with you concerning those quotes from that book, but I do not appreciate your rush to judgment of me based on what someone else said in a book."

All I could say was, "I apologize. I'm sorry."

We spent the next half-hour sharing experiences related to the quotes from the book. Among the things he shared was an experience he had had with a college professor, a friend of his. He and his wife had been invited for dinner and the evening at this professor's home. The professor had three children, all boys.

Mr. S. described that evening by saying, "My wife and I spent the evening dodging the toys those boys were throwing and trying to carry on an intelligent conversation during all of the screaming and foul, angry words they were firing at each other. The only words our friend ever spoke to those boys that entire evening was, 'Tone it down a little.'

He then said nearly the same words to us that you read in the book, 'I believe in allowing children to express them selves.'

My wife and I went home that night wondering what those kids are going to be like when they are grown up."

Of all the sins and offenses I have had to confront as a pastor whom God had called and instructed to reprove and rebuke, those involving jealousy, anger, and bitterness were the most difficult and dangerous. Those ugly traits appeared in our first parent's family in *GENESIS 4*. The end result was **murder.**

When jealousy and anger turn to bitterness, and worse yet, when bitterness turns to hate, it takes a miracle from God to deliver such a person. The biggest problem is that such a person always feels justified in the way he or she feels. The jealousy, anger, bitterness, and hate are someone else's fault. Something he, she, or they did made me this way, and they have my wrath coming.

You would think that those who have the Blessed Holy Spirit shedding the Love of God abroad in their hearts (*ROMANS 5:5*) could never fall prey to such ugly traits, but I can tell you that it does happen. At least it happens to those who profess to believe in Christ. Whether or not they are our Heavenly Father's children, only He knows.

I have seen this anger and bitterness in homes many times; husbands toward wives and wives toward husbands and children toward parents and parents toward children. I have seen it get so bad that years go by without members of the family having any kind of communication with one another.

I grew up as a witness to the worst case of anger, bitterness, and hard hearts that I've not seen equaled since. The pain and grief inflicted on many as the result of two peoples' responses to each others' angry, bitter attitudes was there for many to endure for more than forty years.

It all began with a beautiful family consisting of a dad, mom, and four children; three boys and a girl. What originally precipitated the anger and bitterness that eventually became hatred and two hardened hearts, before I became a witness to the sordid affair, I do not know. No one of the four children seemed to know either. My father, who was one of those four children, said all he remembered was that his father and mother began fighting, each blaming the other for their anger that turned into hatred for each other. According to what he told me, they fought domestically and then legally until their home and everything they owned was lost. They farmed out their children, and then they went their separate ways, never to speak to each other again (My father lived many of those early years with his grandparents).

All of this took place more than twenty years before I arrived on the scene, but my first recollection of all of this was when I asked why Grandpa and Grandma never came to visit us together. That is when my father explained the things that had happened in his home back when he was a child, about my age, at that time. The tears ran down his cheeks as he recounted the story to me.

That was not the only time I saw those tears, for I saw them again some years later at Uncle Chuck's funeral service. They were not the tears shed as he listened to the funeral message or the tears he shed as the casket was lowered into the ground that touched me. It was the tears he shed as he sobbed and pleaded with his father and mother (my grandpa and grandma) to just say something to each other, as they rode from the funeral home to the cemetery. There they both sat, in the back seat of our car, looking stoically, straight ahead, refusing, not only to speak to each other, but refusing to even look at each other.

I was not yet a Christian at that time, but as a boy of sixteen, I could not understand how two people could be like that at their first-born's funeral. Uncle Chuck was only forty-eight years old. Surely their minds went back to that happy moment when he first arrived in their home those forty-eight years before.

Even so, that is not the end of Grandpa's and Grandma's bitterness toward each other. The same scenario was repeated at my father's funeral seven years later. I saw my Grandpa cry uncontrollably when I informed him of my dad's (his second oldest son) sudden death. He sat beside that casket, which back in those days was in our house for two days and two nights. He shed many tears, saying repeatedly that it was the last time he would ever be with his son.

I, along with others who were there, tried to explain that his son was not there, but that he was with the Lord and that was just the body in which he had lived for fifty-two years, but to no avail. He just cried all the more; tears of unbelief.

The next day, the day of Dad's funeral, there were no tears, no words, and no emotions whatsoever as Grandpa and Grandma rode together from our home to the cemetery. It was a repeat of Uncle Chuck's funeral seven years before.

If there are tears shed in heaven, I am sure there were plenty flowing from my father's eyes as his earthly tabernacle was being hauled to its final resting place to await the trumpet sound. I do know that there were tears in his son's eyes; the one who is now penning these lines. In fact there is a lump in my throat as I recall that day, more than fifty years ago.

I was not there for Uncle Steward's or Aunt Amanda's funerals over the next five years, but I was told by my mother who was there, that the scenario with Grandpa and Grandma was the same. Yes, they outlived all four of their children, and both died without ever speaking a word to each other; not even at the gravesides of their four children.

Why do I record this ugly account of my grandparents' anger, bitterness, and hard hearted lives toward each other? Simply to show what the end results will be, of refusing *to "Let ALL bitterness, and wrath, and anger, and clamor, and evil speaking, be put away from you, with all malice," (EPHESIANS 4:31).*

The second reason is, to hopefully, get all of us to recognize the seriousness of the danger to home, family, or God's Family, if God's Remedy is not implemented before hearts are hardened and many innocent suffer.

What is God's Remedy?

"Be ye kind one to another, tenderhearted, forgiving, one another, even as God, for Christ's sake, hath forgiven you," (EPHESIANS 4:32).

"Be not overcome by evil, but overcome evil with good," (ROMANS 12:21).

"...Lord, how many times shall my brother sin against me, and I forgive him? Till seven times?"
"Jesus sayeth unto him, 'I say not unto thee until seven times; but, until seventy times seven," (MATTHEW 18:21, 22).

God's Remedy is Forgiveness, deserved or undeserved. I know my Lord's forgiving **me** was totally undeserved, and I am not about to withhold it from anyone who sins against me.

That ancient enemy of our blessed Heavenly Father and His Beloved Son, our Saviour, is ever busy sowing his seeds of discord in flesh and blood families, and as well, in His spiritual family, the Church.

A shepherd and co-laborer with God must be ever alert to root out these seeds of discord before they take root and spread, but there will always be some that are not caught in time and develop into full bloom anger, bitterness, and even hatred.

Here are just a few representative cases where God, through His Word, granted forgiveness and healing, and several, like Grandpa and Grandma, that went with them to the grave. Only in the last case will I give the details that make for interesting reading, for the primary focus of this book is what God is doing in peoples' lives as He *transforms* His own *"...from glory to glory..." (II CORINTHIANS 3:18),* not merely interesting reading. The important thing is to see and understand that there is forgiveness, deliverance, cleansing, and restoration through His Living Word, even from the vilest sins and the most vehement attacks of the Evil One.

The songwriter surely understood the details so many times involved in rescuing a straying sheep from one of Satan's snares, especially the snares of anger, bitterness, and hatred. Unless and until God grants repentance to one in one of those snares and that one recognizes the terrible state he is in, he will remain ensnared. As a shepherd and co-laborer with God I have spent untold hours pleading, begging, praying, and turning from one scripture to another over weeks until the Truth finally set the ensnared one free.

> *"None of those ransomed ever knew*
> *How deep were the waters crossed,*
> *Nor how dark the night our Lord passed through*
> *Ere He found His sheep that was lost."*

Most rescuing is not done in the counseling room nor in the pastor's study, even though there is nothing wrong with these places. The fact is, straying or ensnared sheep do not very often come to these places for help, forgiveness, or deliverance. As an under-shepherd and a co-laborer with God, we must be willing to go with Him through some of the most trying, difficult, even impossible situations, to free that lost, straying sheep or sometimes two sheep, trapped in the same snare. In the case of an angry father and mother, it is usually with fearful children huddled in the corner, feeling guilty and blaming themselves for the ugliness they see between Dad and Mom. With God's family (the Church) the same principle applies. A co-laborer with God becomes a *peacemaker,* endeavoring *"...to keep the unity of the Spirit in the bonds of peace...,"* by putting the fire out before an angry, bitter spirit spreads throughout the body.

<u>CASE # 1</u>

"Those damn women! They're destroying this church. They succeeded in getting rid of the last pastor, and when they get tired of you, they'll do the same with you." Those were the words of a man who had been a leader in times past in the church of which I was the pastor. They were spoken in my living room, by a man I had spoken to several times before, about his bitter spirit. His mind was so bothered about those women that he had come again, in the middle of the night, to warn me of what I had to look forward to from them.

As in times before, I lovingly, but firmly, warned him about his angry, bitter spirit that was destroying him. This time we got down on our knees as he pleaded with God to forgive him, and when we rose from our knees, there was a smile on his face. My heart was shouting, "Victory! Victory! Praise to our God," but that victory was short-lived, for within minutes, he brought up the name of one of those women. He insisted that something had to be done about those women, and within five minutes he exited my door, muttering those same words he had spoken when he had entered twenty minutes before, **"Those damn women."**

I went back upstairs, told my wife what had just transpired downstairs, and then just lay there until morning, praying and meditating. I kept asking myself, "What happened to this man to fill him with so much anger, bitterness, and hate? How could he seem so repentant one minute and so bitter the next? Is he mentally unstable, or is he just expressing his fallen sin nature? Could it be demonic?"

To this day, I do not have all the answers to these questions, but there is one thing I do know for sure, and that is this: Any time I hear, or even hear of, a professing Christian speak angrily of another Christian, I hurt down inside. From a search of God's Word, I believe this is the same hurt the Holy Spirit feels when we read of Him being grieved in *EPHESIANS 4:30.* Read carefully, the two verses that follow. *"Let all bitterness, and wrath, and anger, and clamor, and evil speaking, be put away from you, with all malice; And be ye kind one to another, tenderhearted, forgiving one another, even as God, for Christ's sake, hath forgiven you,"* (*EPHESIANS 4:31, 32*). Whether or not that man was ever freed from his anger and bitterness, I do not know, but it was still there the last time I saw him. That was more than twenty years after I prayed with him, that night we knelt together in my living room.

I also know what God says about refusing to love our brothers in Christ, as clearly stated in *I JOHN 4:20,* where we read, *"If a man says, I love God, and hateth his brother, HE IS A LIAR; for he that loveth not his brother, whom he hath seen, how can he love God, whom he hath not seen?"*

Through all those years, while I was a shepherd of several of God's local Flocks, I have had several of His Sheep direct their anger and bitterness toward me personally. I do not know that any hated me, but I do know that some became so angry with me that they wished that I would leave. Here is one of those cases.

CASE # 2

"You're the problem. You wrote and asked me what my problem was. Well, I'm telling you, you're the problem!" Those angry words were spoken to me after a Sunday morning service. They came from a man who I thought was one of my best friends and co-laborers with Christ, up until a week before that morning. I spoke of him in my previous book, "Fifty Years A Country Pastor (Shepherd)." His name was Charles.A week prior to that incident, another man in the church had informed me that Charles did not like me and that he had been praying that God would move either him or me. As I said in that book, "Few words from anyone hurt more." I just could not believe that Charles felt that way about me.

He had moved away several months before, and I immediately wrote a letter to him, lovingly stating that whatever there was between us, we needed to deal with it. Here it was, the Sunday after I had mailed that letter, and there was Charles, with his family, sitting in a pew, three rows from the front. As I shook his hand at the door after the service, I asked him to stay until everyone else had gone.

After the last person had walked out the door, I looked over at Charles and calmly asked, "Well Charles, what is our problem?" That is when those angry words, like darts, came from Charles's lips.

I could not believe my ears. This was not the Charles I knew, so my reply was, "You're going to have to explain, because I do not know what you are talking about."

He answered with more angry words. "It's just everything! Your wife..., your daughter..., you have favorites in the church; mostly those new people and — —. The only way you and your wife are ever going to straighten this out is to have each of the families of the church over to the parsonage after the evening services. People are hurt! Another thing, you are doing outside work again, and with the sermons you are preaching, no one will ever be saved."

On and on he ranted, and then came his final words. "I'm moving back here, and I want you to know that I'll be keeping my eye on you." Then, looking out the window toward the parsonage, he continued with, "Right there is one thing that is not good. Your daughter's boyfriend is spending way too much time around here! **That is not good!"**

When he was finished, about all I could say was, "Charles, there's little I can, or want to do about any of the things you have just said. As far as my preaching and teaching of God's Word, that I cannot change. I just want you to know, I am trusting God to restore our relationship to what it was when I came here as your pastor. One last thing I must say for your own and the church's good. You have become angry and bitter, and these things are destructive." I prayed and we departed to our homes.

Months passed and the best I can say is that Charles tolerated me. When he did speak to me, his words were cold. In his eyes, it was the church that was cold, especially me.

Incidentally, when any of God's children grow cold, angry, and bitter; in their minds, it is always others that are at fault. Someone did something that made them angry and bitter. Their flawed reasoning is, *"Until they make things right, I'm just going to be angry and bitter."*

Then one evening Charles called and wanted to talk to me. He sounded different on the phone; very calm and subdued. He came right up that evening and we met at the church. His first words were, "Pastor, will you forgive me?"

I responded with, "I have no problem forgiving you, but first, I must know what I am forgiving you for."

Here is his testimony, from a tender, broken heart. "Last weekend, several of us went to hear L. C. speak at a Christian Life Seminar held at Central B. Church. Everything he said was exactly what you have been teaching. I guess I just needed to hear it from someone else. His messages were exactly the same as yours on *"The Fruit of the Spirit" and "The Gifts of the Spirit."* Then he asked the questions: 'Is your life one of fruit-bearing and service for God's Glory in your home, at the office, on the job, wherever you are, and not merely at church? Do the ones you are around each day see the Fruit of the Spirit: *love, joy, peace, longsuffering, gentleness, goodness, faithfulness, meekness, and self-control*, flowing from your life?'

"It was at that moment that I saw the ugly, old self others had been seeing in me, and I'm asking you to forgive me for being angry toward you and blaming you for the way I thought the church was going. It was not you, it was not my family, and it was not my job. *It was me!*

I felt that everything was going bad everywhere I lived and that it was someone else's fault. I would like to get up in front of the church and confess my sin and apologize to anyone I might have hurt."

When I saw his demeanor and heard his breaking voice, I knew the old Charles was back. I said, "That is fine with me, if you are sure that is what you want to do. I am sure God would be honored." We prayed together, looking forward to Sunday.

Charles followed through that next Sunday evening. Afterward, another person came to me privately and said she, too, was sorry for the hurt she had caused with her bitter attitude. As nearly as I can recall, she said, "I don't want to grow into a bitter, old woman with feelings toward you or anyone else. I want to be who God saved me to be."

The following Sunday evening, two teenage girls sang a duet. Before they sang, they said they wanted to thank the Lord for the change in their parents. One girl was Charles's daughter and the other one was the daughter of the lady just mentioned above.

That was thirty-five years ago, and God is still working in the lives of their descendants, to the third generation. God has given me the privilege of watching Him work, through His Word, in not only the lives of the parents, but in their children and grandchildren as well. Some are on the foreign mission field, and others are some of my closest friends and brothers and sisters in Christ.

"Ye have not chosen me, but I have chosen you, and ordained you, that ye should go and bring forth fruit, and that your fruit should remain (abide)..." (JOHN 15:16).

What would have happened if Charles had remained in his bitter life? Only God knows, but we do know that God does not allow His children to live that way **(read** *HEBREWS 12:1-15*).

The question might be asked, "Wasn't it painful to have those who were angry and bitter toward you, their pastor?" Yes, I would be lying if I said I never had the feeling that I wished they would just go away, but I knew that feeling was not from my Heavenly Father. He did not want them to go away. He just wanted them to come back to Him. His heart ached, and through His Word, He brought them through a bitter experience, to a lifetime of glory and honor to Himself. By sharing His grief and receiving from Him His grace and love, instead of old Adam's revengeful nature, look at what a great work I saw God do, and He continues to do to this day.

I could include many more cases where God granted repentance and restoration between husbands and wives, parents and children, brothers and sisters, and even pastors and sheep, but let us look at just one more case and we will call this case HANK.

CASE # 3
"HANK"

"Pastor Walter, come quick! Hank just shot himself!" I received that telephone call one summer evening, just after dark. Without hesitation I ran for my car, with my wife pleading for me not to go.

Wait, let us back up a little. I am starting in the middle of an on-going situation filled with anger and bitterness that I thought had reached its climax, so let's back up a bit. Hank and I had become somewhat close the night he shared his innermost feelings that included his anger, bitterness, and, yes, even hate, with me. That night was nearly three years earlier, and since then we had had a half dozen or more of what we would call "counseling sessions" today. Hank was even occasionally seen in one of our church services. He claimed to be a staunch believer in Christ, and I had no reason to doubt his faith, except for the angry, bitter spirit he had toward his wife.

He told me how he, his wife and their children used to go to church and Sunday school together. He said he had even taught a Sunday school class, but this had all ended abruptly some years before. According to him, his wife and children were again attending another church, but he could not go with them because of something that had taken place in this relationship, which, even the thought of it was unbearable to him. With some of the most painful words I have ever heard from anyone, he told me this story.

"When I went to the war my girlfriend, who is now my wife and I were engaged. We corresponded throughout those years I was away, making plans for our future home together, and when I came home we were happily married. We were both Christians, and as I said, we were active in church together through all the years when our children were born.

"Then it happened! A man from the town where we lived before the War, came up to me at work. What he told me that day could not have hurt worse if he had taken out a gun and shot me!"

With those words, Hank choked up, almost unable to say any more. After waiting a few seconds he was able to continue. "'You're Hank —this man asked?"

"I replied, 'Yes.'"

"You're married to Carrie — ?"

"Again I replied, 'Yeah.'"

"Then he said, 'She's some girl. I lived with her for almost a year during the war.'

100

"I just stood there, stunned. I could see by the look on his face that he thought I knew all about their affair. I just walked away, and later that evening I faced my wife, just mentioning the man's name.

"She just started to cry, saying, 'I'm sorry! I'm so sorry!'

"At that moment I hated her. I just went out and got drunk. All I could think was that I was married to a woman that had played the part of a whore in her father's house," (*DEUTERONOMY 22:21*). After he told me this story, he hesitated, waiting for my reaction.

This was not the first time I had heard similar stories and there certainly have been more than one since then. Probably there will be some who read these lines and remember similar situations I am recalling right now. *In most of those situations God in His Grace granted forgiveness, deliverance, and restoration, by giving each one the GRACE to forgive the other*. **Take the time to read that sentence again.** That is our Heavenly Father's method of dealing with sins between two of his children, whether it be husband and wife or between two brothers or sisters in Christ.

Those who have read this book from the beginning remember what Cham said to me, with his unfaithful wife seated beside him. "Yes, I can and will forgive her. I have not always been the perfect husband either..." You see, he knew he needed God's grace and forgiveness, and, at times, Minnie's as well.

Hank had his own problems, and as I did not respond to his hesitation, he continued by asking me, "How would you feel if your wife did something like this?"

I quickly responded, "Like you do, somewhere between angry and bitter."

"What would you do if you were me?"

"I know what I should do if this happened with my wife, but I have never been there, so I do not know what I would do."

What do you mean by that?" he asked.

"Let me ask you a question before I tell you what I should do if I was in your situation. First, has your wife ever been unfaithful since you have been married?"

He answered with an emphatic, "No."

"Second, you said she cried and said she was sorry. Do you think she was and still is sorry?"

"Maybe, but it's a little late for that. Why didn't she think of that before she did what she did, or at least, why didn't she tell me about it before we were married?"

"I cannot answer your first question, but think I know the answer to the second."

"O.K., why didn't she tell me before we were married?"

"That is simple. She loved you and was afraid you would not marry her if she told you about the affair."

"What kind of reasoning is that? If she loved me, why did she do what she did while I was overseas?"

"I told you I did not have the answer to that question. All I know is that a lot of girls and even married women did what your wife did, including my sister."

He quickly responded, "Yes, and so did King David in the Bible. Even worse than that, he had her husband killed so he could marry her." There was no doubt, he knew his Bible *(II SAMUEL 11 and 12).*

"Now, you asked me what I would do if I was in your shoes, and here is my answer. For my Lord's Name Sake, for the good of my wife, and, as well, my own peace of mind, I should forgive my wife, and never bring the whole affair up to her again."

"You're saying I should do that!"

"Yes, and not only do I say that, but that is what God says you should do as well. *'...Forgive and ye shall be forgiven,'* is the way our Lord put it in *LUKE 6:37.'*"

Hank responded to those words, almost in anger, "Why should I forgive her, and why do you say I need to be forgiven? She's the guilty one!"

"Hank, you are the one with the biggest problem. You have given in to these horrible feelings of anger, bitterness, and hate. To yield to them is SIN of the most destructive kind. They are destroying you and are bound to spread to your children."

Although Hank did not understand what God was trying to show him, and was determined to retain his anger and bitterness toward his wife, he did keep coming to see me. At times, he blamed me for taking sides with his wife, with whom I had talked just one time. She knew she had done wrong and also knew she was now reaping the consequences of her past sins, even though she had confessed those sins and knew God had forgiven her.

Every so often, Hank went to the bottle to try to drown those awful feelings of anger and bitterness that rose up whenever he thought of his wife's past sins and of her keeping them from him. All of which leads up to the night Hank's wife called me with that desperate plea, "Come quick Hank just shot himself."

As I drove to Hank's and Carrie's home, I was literally trembling, not knowing what I was going to find when I arrived. I also did not know that Hank's wife had called my house immediately after I had left, telling my wife that I didn't need to come. Hank had come home drunk, gotten his gun, gone out into the darkness, and fired into the air, pretending to commit suicide. Within minutes, he had come back into the house, put the gun away, and had gone back outside to his workshop at the end of the garage. That is where he was when I pulled into the driveway.

As the garage door was already open, I walked right in. "What's going on out here, Hank?" I inquired.

As I spoke those words, Hank picked up a hammer, turned, and started toward me with the hammer raised. I had no time to do anything except raise my arms in self-defense. Speaking with slurred drunken words he said, "I could split your head wide open—. Then he dropped the hammer, threw his arms around me, and finished his sentence, "...but I love you too much to hurt you."

After that incident, I warned Hank about his drinking. I knew it was not a habitual thing, but it was evident that when he did have a few drinks he could be dangerous.

To my knowledge, he never touched alcohol for the next four years. During that time he came regularly to our church services, and his wife and children attended a church some ten miles in the opposite direction.

There were no more problems with alcohol, but the bitterness remained, and occasionally, when Hank brought it up, I reminded him what God's Word says, saying, *"Forgiveness, Hank, forgiveness."*

I believe Hank understood what God was saying to him, but did not understand that the power to choose against those awful feelings comes from a Loving Father who has forgiven us.

That is not the end of this story. I moved away from that pastorate and Hank and his wife also moved, to another state. I had almost forgotten about Hank, except on occasion as I was interceding (praying) for members of God's flock, his name crossed my mind. This same thing has happened and continues to happen for dozens of the Heavenly Shepherd's flock that I have had occasion to minister to in years gone by.

Some fifteen years passed, and one evening our telephone rang. The voice at the other end of the line asked, "Are you the Pastor Walter who used to be the pastor in — ?"

When I told her I was the one and the same, she said a man named Hank had asked her if she could get my address for him. I gave her the address, wondering why Hank would want it.

About two weeks later, I received this letter:

"Grace won out. Forgiveness granted, anger and bitterness gone, no alcohol for many, many years. My wife and I have been attending church together for several years, after nearly thirty years of attending separate churches. Just thought you would like to know.

In Christ,
Hank

P. S. Speaking of Forgiveness, Please forgive me for all the trouble I caused you."

Hank, you are forgiven, and thanks for the tears of joy your letter brought to this shepherd's heart.

SECTION THREE

Bad Things That Did Not Happen

B efore we talk about those bad things that did not happen, let us take a painful look at bad things that will always come our way. They are part and parcel of living in a fallen creation. Until God has completed His work of Redemption and restoration these bad things will be with us. They hurt and leave us with the question "why" that has no answer. The only thing for us to do when any of them touch us personally is to hand them over to our Sovereign God who "works all things after the counsel of His own will." Whether He causes them to happen or just allows them come our way makes little difference.

To what are we referring? In my former book I called them Traumatic Events in A Country Pastor's Life. In Romans 8:18 Paul calls them "the sufferings of this present time." Without the comfort of knowing these things are temporary and "not worthy of the Glory that shall be revealed in us" all we are left with is the plaguing question "WHY?"

Why did Willis, a fifty two year old father and husband in perfect health suddenly die doing his morning chores?

Why all those accidents that took Belden, Joe, Joy and a host of others from us in their prime of life?

Why does the most godly woman I have ever known lose her first husband in a mine cave in, have her first son drown at age thirteen, her mother die suddenly in her arms, have the intolerable care

105

of her senile father the last two years of his life, have her second husband die of cancer at age fifty two, and finally she herself die in excruciating pain with a terminal disease?

Why does Vicki, a loving thirty eight year old wife and mother die suddenly leaving Kermit and her two children behind when at the same time Irene in her seventies develops Alzheimer's and for the past thirteen years lies there in that nursing home in a vegetative state?

Why does Luther, a brilliant defender of Creation Science (whom God used in my life and ministry) die of cancer when his ministry was so needed?

Why? Why? Why? The list of bad things goes on and on. We can not avoid them, but they are not the bad things we are talking about in this chapter. We are talking about the bad things that <u>did not</u> happen. You don't understand? Read on, you will.

It was New Years Eve. Many families would be getting together to celebrate an evening of fun and games which was good. For anyone who wished to come, a group of us would meet at the church for a service with refreshments following. This would be a different kind of service. No preaching, no planned program. The only thing I had asked of those who would come was to have one thing to thank the Lord for that happened during the past year and one thing they would like Him to do the coming year.

There were not very many there that night, but what a blessed night for those who did come. One after another expressed their thankfulness for God's goodness, for material provisions, for healings, one for a new grandchild, another for a new family in the church, etc. All good things, and for the most part looking forward to more of the same for the next year. With the pianist at the piano we would sing a verse or two of a song that would come to mind interspersed with our testimonies of thanksgiving and praise.

I was the last to express my thankfulness. Taking a list of fifteen or twenty things I had compiled out of my pocket, I started with these words: "I want to thank our wonderful Lord for all the things that did not happen this past year." They were all things that had happened during years past. Then with everyone wondering what was coming I began to read.

1. No marriages broke up, no divorces.
2. No out of wedlock pregnancies.
3. No one got miffed and left our church family.
4. No one caused disunity by a critical spirit.
5. No one went off into false doctrine.
6. No one started false rumors.
7. To my knowledge, no one is holding a grudge.
8. None of our young people got into drugs or alcohol.
9. No one was manifesting a "holier than thou" attitude.
10. No roots of bitterness took root and spread to others.
11. No blood family feuds over money or inheritances, etc.
12. No warring actions in the church about who was going to run things.

After reading a few more things on the list we gathered in a circle around the church auditorium. Holding hands we prayed. We thanked God for the many blessings of the year that just passed and asked for many good things that could honor Him during the coming year. Most of all we thanked Him for the bad things that did not happen and prayed for more of the same not to happen the coming year. "Father I do not pray that you should take them out of the world but that you should keep them from the evil one."

PRACTICING PREVENTIVE PRAYER

There is an old adage that all of us have heard many times: "An ounce of prevention is worth a pound of cure." Although not found verbatim in the Scriptures the principle involved runs all through the Bible.

In the physical realm we all know that proper food; (in proper amounts) rest and exercise would prevent many of our physical ailments. Even in the mechanical realm proper maintenance prevents many future breakdowns. And there is no place this is truer than in a local church and in each individual Christians Life. I grew up in a church that depended upon the "annual revival" to keep it from dying spiritually and morally. And what excitement there was when the altar was lined with reclaimed backsliders, (more times than not, the same ones that lined the altar the year before and the same ones that would line it again next year.) For anyone to imply there was anything wrong with this was heresy. To suggest that the need for a revival could have been prevented by proper preaching, teaching, counseling and praying which would keep those who know Jesus Christ *"growing in Grace and Knowledge ofHim"* day by day, instead of *"being led away with the error of the wicked."* (*II Peter 3:17-18*) would be looked upon with much skepticism.

Our subject here is Preventative Prayer, prayers that if God answers there will be little need for corrective prayer, and we are primarily talking about the spiritual realm. If we pray regularly for one another the prayer our Lord prayed for us that night before "Calvary" *"Father keep them from the Evil one"* and God answers that prayer, we won't have to do a lot of corrective praying and counseling to get one or more of us out of the *"snare of the devil whom he has taken captive."*

Following is a list of requests in our Lords and the Apostle Paul's Prayers. How many of them are corrective and how many of them are preventative?

1. *"Lead us not into temptation, but deliver us from evil"* Matt. 6:13.

2. *"Father, keep them from the Evil One" Jn. 17:15 "Father, Sanctify them through thy Truth, Thy Word is Truth."* Jn.17:17

3. *"Father make them one, as thou, Father, art in me and I in Thee, that they also may be one is us." Jn;17:21*

4. *"Father of Glory give unto this church the Spirit of Wisdom and Revelation in the Knowledge of Yourself."*
   "Enlighten the eyes of this churches understanding,
   (1) "That this church (and each individual) might know what is the Hope of his Calling."
   (2) "That this church might know what the riches of the Glory of His Inheritance in the Saints."
   (3) "That this church might know what is the exceeding greatness of HIS power to us who believe"

Compare Paul's Prayers *in Eph. 3:16-21 - Phil. 1:8-11 - Col. 1:9-13- I Thess. 3:11-13 - I Thess.1: 11-12*

Speaking out of a Pastors heart, let me just say it is much more pleasant to meet with the church board for prayer and be able to pray that God would fill our hearts with His Love and His Wisdom and impart to us a knowledge of His Will in the decisions we need to make in the operation of a local church, then it is to meet together, discuss all the *"roots of bitterness"* that were spreading, or *"the murmurings and disputings"* (criticisms) usually over nothing, and then plead with God to help us to know what to do about them, or asking Him to deal with the individuals that were causing all the trouble.

Preventing bad things from happening is much better and easier than correcting them after they have happened, and furthermore our Loving Heavenly Father surely finds more joy in seeing His children *walk in Truth* than in correcting them when they don't. And he does do that also. *111 John 4* and *Heb. 12:6.*

LEARNING TO PRAY

"Bless the Lord O my soul; and all that is in me, bless your holy name. Bless the Lord, O my soul, and let me not forget all your benefits."

I first heard those words from the lips of an old missionary from Africa. About twenty of us young pastors and this man all knelt among the pews of this little country church. His words were loud. I knew he could not have his head bowed like the rest of us kneeling between those pews. As he was straight across from me I turned my head and sneaked a peak at him.

There he was on his knees with face and hands raised toward heaven, eyes wide open with tears running down his face, praying what I later knew was Psalm 103.

At first glance I thought, "What is this man doing?" But before he finished I noticed tears in my eyes too. As we arose from our knees most of us were reaching for our handkerchiefs to wipe our tears away. It was right there I learned what worship praying was all about. We had all prayed; He worshiped. That was more than fifty years ago and one of my regrets is that I never had the love for God, boldness, or whatever it was that missionary had, which I lacked, to worship publicly like he did that day. He was not a Pharisee praying publicly to be seen of men. He was a Daniel praying to his God at his open window for all to see and hear even though his public praying might land him in the lion's den.

"O Lord burden us to pray, burden us to pray, burden us to pray! Burden us for the lost, burden us to pray for one another! Burden us until we must tell others about you. Burden us... on and on," getting more emotional with each phrase. The one who prayed this way got so fervent that at times his son was embarrassed when any of his friends were with him at a church service where his father prayed publicly. But his son knew his father meant every word he spoke and he also knew he was pleading with his God he believed in and wanted to obey with all his being. He not only prayed like this in prayer meetings. His son heard him more than once in the middle of the night praying just as fervently. "O God get hold of my boys, get hold of my boys, get hold of my boys before they get out into sin, O God please get...

God did get hold of that father's boys in answer to his prayers just as He had gotten hold of a man named Frank some years before. Frank was this father's two boys Sunday School teacher. You never saw two happier men than that father and Frank the night the older of those two boys and his girlfriend came forward and publicly confessed Christ as their Lord and Saviour.

Several years after that, the father of those boys died. That was more than fifty years ago. Frank lived for forty four more years. That boy that came forward with his girlfriend all those years ago had only seen Frank several times during those forty four years, the last time several years before he died.

At that meeting here is what Frank said, "Jimmie, it is sure good to see you. Your daddy taught me to pray. I've prayed faithfully for all you boys in that Sunday School class down through the years and still do. All of you boys are saved now. (You, Harry, Wayne, Red, Warren, Ray, Bobby, and Ivan)

After talking and reminiscing for a half hour or so, Frank took out his wallet and handed Jimmie a hundred dollar bill with these words; "Use this however God directs you." He had sent Jimmie twenty dollar bills at least ten times during the years he was studying for the ministry nearly fifty years before that last meeting.

What did I learn about prayer from the father of those two boys and from Frank, their Sunday School teacher? From the father of those boys I learned what God meant when He said, "The **fervent**

prayer of a righteous man availeth much."(*James 5:16*) That father's **fervent** praying literally prayed his son to the Lord and into a lifetime of ministry. From Frank's praying I leaned what **faithful** prayer is all about. At that last meeting with Frank, Jimmie was near seventy and Frank was well on his way toward ninety. Nearly sixty years of praying for those boys in that Sunday School class, I can hardly imagine such **faithfulness.**

How did I come to know so much about Frank and the father of those two boys who he said taught him to pray? That answer is easy. I am Jimmie, one of that father's two boys.

From that old missionary to Africa I learned what worshiping in prayer was all about. From my father I saw what fervent praying could accomplish and from Frank, my Sunday School teacher, I learned what faithfulness and persevering in prayer was all about.

I've learned a lot about prayer from books on that subject and from hearing other godly saints pray, but the prayer from which I have learned the most is found in John 17. In this chapter The Holy Spirit directed John to record the most intimate of relationships. Deity speaks to Deity. The Eternal Son speaks to His Eternal Father. The subject is those who are dearest to his heart; His disciples and those who would believe in Him through their word down through the centuries (Including you and me.) They (we) are His Church.

At the beginning of His public ministry He taught his disciples to pray. Here in John Seventeen He is not only praying to His Father about you and me. He is allowing us to listen in, thereby teaching us who we are, and how to pray for His OWN; (children of the Father, gifts to the Son). We are truly on holy ground. Let us take off our earthly shoes, shut out the ungodly world that surrounds us and quietly listen, learn, and worship. As we listen closely we will learn three vital lessons that apply to the third and final section of this book entitled God Is Busy Fixing Things. There are many lessons to be learned in the entire chapter. The three we want to learn here are in verses 14-17.

First we hear The Son say to his Father, "they are not of the world even as I am not of the world" and He repeats the same words in verse 16. His Own, His Disciples, His Church, you and I, if we are truly believers and not merely members of a religious organization; just as He, we are not of this world.

Secondly we hear Him pray for us. "Father I do not pray that you should take them out of the world but that you should keep them from the evil one." From Genesis three to this present moment the evil one, the prince of this world has been exerting all of his subtle wiles to defeat our Father's purpose of having a people who are one with Him. That is you and I who are believers, or as he says seven times in this chapter; "gifts of the Father to the Son." (vs. 2,6,9,11,12,24)

Thirdly He prays for us who are not of this world to be sanctified; hear His words; "*Father sanctify them through thy truth: thy word is truth.*"

If only we who claim to believe in Him and believe His word is truth would walk in that truth and really live as strangers and pilgrims here, looking ever to Jesus the author and finisher of our faith. And if this is to ever be a reality in a local church we must learn to pray as He prayed for us that dark night, the night before the day of His crucifixion. Hear those words again, and let us learn to pray for ourselves as He prayed for us, each one from His heart praying, "*Father keep me from the evil one, sanctify me through your truth, your word is truth.*" If He answers that prayer we will not have to go through many of the things we spoke about in the first two sections of this book. **A lot of bad things would not happen.**

As with everything our God does, he does these two blessed things the same way for those who are on this pilgrimage through the enemy's territory on their way to Glory. Through His word He keeps us from the evil one and sanctifies us continually. He does not do this through His Word that remains on the pages of His Book, but by that Word He instills in our minds and hearts as we faithfully open His Word and eat it as our daily food. It is His Word *that we hide in our hearts that keeps us from sinning against Him. (Psalm 119:11)*. It is that same Word His saints use to defeat the evil one. It is the "*sword of the Spirit*" (*Ephesians 6:17*) before which Satan cannot stand. It is the sanctifying Word that as we regularly open His Book to see and know Him that we are constantly *being changed from glory I to glory. (II Corinthians 3:18)*

As a pastor and God's co-worker I learned early that the more I could get His people in His word and His word in the hearts and minds of His people the less I would have to confront sin in their lives. Added to this, more of us spending more time in the prayer closet praying preventive prayer, there would be a whole lot of **bad things that would not happen.** Sometimes even a bad thing would turn out to be used by God to produce some good things. "**A Thief in Our Youth Group**" was one of those times.

Danny
A Thief in Our Church Youth Group?

The other day, as we were closing the picnic house for the winter, I took a look at the old electric stove we used to prepare our picnic meals several times each summer. That stove sure has been around. We bought it new fifty-five years ago when we moved to our first pastorate. It has been with us wherever we have lived since then. Every time I see it, memories flood my mind. This time I thought of Danny as I looked at the little repaired spot I had fixed when the enamel had been chipped nearly forty-five years ago.

"What does that repaired chip have to do with Danny, and who is Danny?" you might ask. Well, Danny was a fifteen...no, let us go back to the beginning and start with that "chipped enamel." We (my wife, two children, and I) had just arrived home from spending Thanksgiving with our families, who lived three hundred miles away. It was late; nearly midnight. After that six hour drive, we just wanted to go directly to bed, but I had to go to the kitchen for a drink of water before turning in for the night, a habit I have had all my life.

As I turned on the kitchen light I saw broken glass all over the kitchen floor. There, in front of the stove, lay a stone. Turning to the left I noticed that the window in the rear entry door was broken. Upon closer examination I surmised what had happened. Someone had thrown that stone through that window. A closer investigation revealed where that stone had gone after coming through the window. A small chip of enamel, no bigger than the end of my little finger nail, lay on the floor in front of the stove.

Now, forty-five years later, I stand here looking at that little spot where that stone hit that stove all those years ago, and that brings me back to the beginning of this story.

We immediately called Perry, our small town police force. He was one of the people I mentioned in a previous chapter; one Floyd insisted that I must go talk to about the Lord. He and I had become good friends since that time.

He was at our house within minutes. Upon arriving, he immediately called for an investigator. He, too, arrived in less than twenty minutes. His first question was, "Is there anything missing?"

We could not find anything missing or other damage done, other than the broken window and the chipped enamel on the stove. His next question was, "How about jewelry or money?"

While Perry and the investigator took pictures and gathered evidence, my family and I went through the house to see if anything was missing. The first one to notice anything was our eight year old daughter. "My piggy bank and youth group money are gone!" she exclaimed, still in her bedroom.

The next words we heard came from our four year old son, "Daddy, my piggy bank is gone, too!" he yelled excitedly.

With further examination, I found that my piggy bank (money my wife and I kept in a jar in the kitchen cupboard for incidentals (mostly change and a few dollar bills) was also missing. We estimated the total amount of money missing to be between forty and fifty dollars.

There was nothing else even out of place, and there was no damage other than the broken window and the chip out of the stove.

The next morning, during our Sunday service, I announced what we had found when we had come home the night before. Over the next several months I talked to Perry three or four times. Each time he said the investigation was continuing. There were many times when someone in the church asked if there was any new information.

By the next spring I had almost put the whole incident out of my mind. Then, one day in April Perry stopped the school bus I was driving, and asked me to get out. I was embarrassed as I had just left the school with a full load of students to deliver to their homes. His only words were, "The reason I asked you to get out is I don't want any of the students to hear what I have to tell you. We have pretty good evidence that a boy in your church broke into your house last fall; Danny B. Let me know what you want me to do."

I knew what he meant by that, as he and I had worked together on several different incidents involving young people in the community. I knew his hope was that he would not have to be involved any further with Danny. He hated to arrest young people. He loved them and always wanted to see each situation solved "justly," without legal justice, if possible. I agreed wholeheartedly on this point.

The title of this section is "**Bad Things That Did Not Happen.**" With Danny, Perry's desire and my prayer were, "Lord, keep a bad thing from getting worse."

Perry knew I would do just that, and I knew it was my Heavenly Father's desire for Danny as well, for Danny had professed faith in Christ not long before this incident took place. I would be dealing with Danny **as a child of God who had committed a sin against his Heavenly Father, not as one who had committed a crime against society.** That is, if Danny was really guilty and was willing to confess his sin. How was I to go about bringing this to pass?

As always, I prayed, "Lord, this is your work. Give me the wisdom I need to deal with Danny."

The next afternoon I drove over to the school and waited until I saw Danny come out and start his walk home. Driving up beside him, I shouted out my car window, "Danny, need a ride home?"

He responded, "Yeah, Thanks."

He got in without looking at me. After driving a few blocks in total silence, I nonchalantly asked, "Danny, is there something you would like to tell me?"

With tears in his eyes he responded, saying, "Pastor, I'm the one who broke into your home. I'm sorry. I've wanted to tell you for a long time, but I spent the money and can't pay you back."

I pulled off onto the side of the road, and we had a heart to heart discussion. There were tears in my eyes as well as in Danny's; tears of fear in Danny's, but tears of abounding joy in mine.

God was working in Danny, and I just wanted to be His co-laborer in what was to be done now. I assured him that I had forgiven him, but it was God's Spirit that made him feel so guilty all those months since he had committed the sin of stealing. Sin is always against God, and it was God alone that would forgive and cleanse if he would confess his sin to Him. This he did right then and there.

Danny's next question was: "Does anyone else need to know about this? Does the youth group at church need to know?"

My answer to him: "Danny, sins have consequences, and that includes forgiven sins. The only people who need to know are your father and mother, and that is where we are going right now so you can tell them."

With those words he really started to cry. "No, no! My dad will beat me! He'll beat me to death!"

"No he won't. I will be right there when you tell them, but there is one more thing you and I need to agree on. You do not have the money to pay me back, so I am asking you if you are willing to work with me around the church and parsonage for forty hours at the rate of $1.00 per hour. We will work together cleaning up the mess left after the hard winter we have just been through." Smiling, I added, "Especially the hard winter you have been through, carrying that heavy load of guilt day after day."

He readily agreed to my offer, and off we went to his home. When we arrived, I am sure his parents were wondering why I was bringing their son home. After the next fifteen minutes, I am sure they were glad it was their pastor and not the police.

I was the first to speak, saying, "Danny and I have just had a good talk together, and he has something to tell you."

With tears still in his eyes, Danny fearfully said, "I'm the one who broke into pastor's house and stole his money."

You never saw two, more shocked people. I saw a mother with a broken heart and anger in his father's eyes. Just like Danny had said, "He will beat me."

He reached into his pocket for his wallet, with a question aimed at me, "How much did he take? I'll take care of him later."

I replied, "Put your wallet away, and please do not do what I think you meant by, 'Taking care of him later.' Danny and I have an agreement whereby he can repay me."

Again in anger, his father responded with, "How can he repay you? He has no money!"

I explained our agreement and assured Danny and his parents that no one would ever know anything about the whole matter, except Perry, our town policeman. I also told them I was sure he would consider the case closed when I told him how we had handled the situation.

Danny and I did spend many hours working together that spring, which was good for both of us. It was all a part of being a co-laborer together with God in building lives and family ties for His Glory.

Probably the greatest blessing I received from it all came several months later when Danny's father came to me and said he was a believer in Christ and wanted to be baptized.

Instead of **a bad thing that did not happen**, the bad thing that Danny did led to good things that God did, not only in Danny, but in his father as well.

I can only imagine the bad things that could have happened if the police would have picked Danny up and arrested him. It would have become public knowledge, a disgrace to his family, a shame to the church, and can you imagine how the youth group of the church would look at Danny after that?

God truly **stopped a lot of bad things from happening**, and for good measure, added a few good things as well.

PRAYER POWER

From one of the authors mentioned in the dedication of this book I learned early in my ministry the power of prayer in the presentation of Gods Word whether given out to hundreds from the pulpit or to individuals in the home or on the street. I have also experienced the powerlessness of proclaiming the Word in "Word only," That author said this, "I am not sure which is more important, speaking to people about God or speaking to God about people. Both are absolute essentials if God is to use His Word to transform lives."

My own experience as a pastor is that I needed as much time in the prayer closet as I did in the study if I was to see God transform lives, not merely make religious people like those described in Romans 2:17-29 and 10:15-21 and Heb 4:1-2. How many there are who are hearers and knowers of Gods Word only, and not believers in and obeyers of the God of the Word, only He knows.

The following account of <u>Larry C</u>. explains the difference between "<u>A Work of God</u>" and Religion.

It was 6:30 a.m. on a Monday morning. My wife and I were ready to leave to go thirty miles to the city to work. We had just moved from the city into this old farmhouse a mile from the church we had been pastoring for more than a year now.

As we were going out the door a man got out of his car and came toward us carrying two dozen eggs. He introduced himself as Larry C. the husband of Mary, and the father of Larry Jr. He handed the eggs to me and at the same time asked me this question: "Can you tell me how I can have my sins forgiven?"

I told him that I could definitely tell him how he could have his sins forgiven, but that I would like to talk with him in a little more detail than we had the time for at the moment. As we were both on our way to work we arranged for a meeting at his home that evening.

All day long as I went around my dry cleaning route I prayed. At that early stage in the ministry I had already learned the absolute necessity of The Holy Spirit to accompany His Word if there was to be any permanent change in the life of the hearer. I was also learning the empowering of the Spirit was received in the prayer closet, not in the study. This day was a day in the prayer closet even though I was running my dry cleaning route. By the time I got home I was dead tired but I could not wait to get together with a <u>man in whom I was sure God was</u> <u>working</u>. A day on the dry cleaning route produced a weary body, but the same day in the prayer closet produced a vibrant spirit. Probably only you co-laborers together with God will understand that paragraph. All who read on will understand when you see the change in Larry.

When I arrived at Larry's home he took the first fifteen minutes to give me the background that led up to his question: "Can you tell me how I can have my sins forgiven?"

He explained to me how he was a fifty three year old man who had not been inside a church building more than half dozen times in his entire life. He said he believed in God but had little knowledge of **"what religion was all about."** (His words) The thing that had gotten him interested was that his wife and young teen age son had started attending our services at this little old country church that we had opened the year before. They had been trying to get him to come along with them but his excuse was that he was not good enough to go to church. They told him how Pastor Walter could tell him how he could become good enough. (Not exactly the way I would have worded it.) That was what led him to come to my door that morning with his question: "Can you tell me how I can have my sins forgiven?"

Now it was my turn. My first words were, do you have a Bible? "Yes it's right here" was his response. "My wife has been trying to show me some things in it." My next question: "Do you believe the

121

Bible is Gods Word?" Again his response: " I guess so. I told you I am pretty ignorant about **religion.**" (It is still **religion** and I'm not here to talk about **religion**)

For the next three hours we turned from one scripture to another beginning with the commission Christ gave to his disciples at his ascension when he said that: "*repentance and forgiveness of sins* should be preached in His name among all nations: *Luke 24:47.*

We then flipped the page to John chapter one where we read about the Living Word, the Creator God, The True Light who became flesh and dwelt among us. Then we turned to all those scriptures that speak of this Ones death on the cross, his burial and resurrection. Then back to John 1:12 where we read that by receiving Him we become His children.

For the remainder of those three hours and over the months that followed we studied the Word together where we saw how that with us in Christ and Christ in us, we not only had our sins forgiven but we had reconciliation with The Father, a perfect standing before Him, new Life now, a Blessed Hope for the future and so much more. God had brought Larry into a living relationship with Himself. His neighbors thought he had gotten religion, as he was one of those who could not keep still about his "new found faith." He wanted others to know Jesus to, and would ask me to go with him to explain from the Bible how they to could know Jesus Christ in a personal way.

God had shown Larry that he not only needed to have his sins forgiven, but that he needed a New life, a New Lord and a New Love. All this he had found in his living relationship with Jesus Christ.

Through this experience with Larry all those years ago God was teaching me that only He could transform a person on the inside. He does that through His Word which He wrote through men of old and empowers as his co-workers allow that Word to dwell in them, and prayerfully proclaim it to others.

"OUR GLORIOUS GOSPEL"

"For we preach not ourselves, but Christ Jesus the Lord, and ourselves your servants for Jesus' sake—We have this treasure in

earthen vessels, that the excellency of the power may be of God and not of us." 11 Cor. 4:5-7

We who are Gods co-workers are simply *"vessels, sanctified and meet for the Master's (The Holy Spirits) use."* The power to transform the Larry's of this fallen race is **in Him Alone.**

Those friends and neighbors may think Larry had just gotten religion but as the Christ who died for our sins and rose again begins to manifest Himself through Larry's character, attitudes, and actions they will begin to see what he has is not merely a religion but **a living relationship with the living God.** ("Transformed by Grace Divine") A transformation that started that day he received Jesus Christ and would continue until he went home to be with Him.

It is sadly true that so many even among those who name the name of Christ have only a religion. Religion is simply made up of Rites, Rituals, Rules and Regulations.

1. Usually a Rite in the past when they say they became a Christian. (Maybe church membership, maybe praying a certain prayer, maybe going forward in a meeting, or being baptized, etc.)
2. Rituals consisting of their Sunday worship and service for God. Usually called "GOING TO CHURCH."
3. Rules and Regulations to govern their conduct throughout the rest of the week. (Mostly bad things a Christian should not do)

The following account of my visit with Mr. Chilson which took place shortly after that with Larry illustrates the difference between entering into a living relationship with God and just going through a religious rite or ritual.

"Mr.Chilson, are you a Christian?"

Mr. Chilson's answer: "I used to be but I am not anymore."

"What do you mean when you say, you used to be but not any more?"

Here is Mr. Chilson's explanation.

"About ten years ago I was gloriously saved at a revival meeting in the P.H. church. I quit smoking and drinking. I even quit telling dirty stories and did my best to quit cursing. For three years I went to church nearly every Sunday and sometimes even to prayer meeting during the week." I said, "That all sounds good. What happened?" Mr. Chilson's explanation "I just quit being a Christian. I went back to smoking, drinking, cursing and all the bad things I did before I was saved. I don't go to church. I'm just not a Christian anymore."

"What do you mean when you say you were saved? What happened to you that night in that revival meeting?" That was my next question

"All I can remember is going to the altar and people praying around me. Then I prayed and I was saved."

My next question "What did you pray that night?"

Mr. Chilson's answer, "I can't remember that far back. Something the preacher told me to pray. Then he told me I was saved."

My next question "Did he show you any thing from the Bible?"

"Not that I remember."

Then I asked: "Why do you say you are not a Christian any more?"

His almost indignant answer: "I told you. I quit being a Christian. I live just like I did before I was saved, so I'm not a Christian anymore."

I took the next half hour or so explaining from Gods Word all the things I had gone over with Larry and so many others both before and after him.

This meeting with Mr. Chilson is typical of dozens, maybe hundreds over the last fifty eight years since I to, knelt at an altar and confessed Jesus as Lord.

Like Mr. Chilson I to quit some bad habits but that was not what made me a Christian. Like Larry the year before I was by faith receiving the Saviour who died for my sin and rose again who would come to live in me and through me. The bad things I quit doing and the good things that replaced them were the results of Gods great salvation (Jesus Christ) living in me. As with Larry I did not have a religion I could quit. God had brought me into an eternal relationship with the Risen Christ that would constantly increase from glory to glory until He would take me home.

For a better understanding of the difference between religion and a living relationship with God read the Appendix in this book. It is four chapters from "Experiencing The Work of The Holy Spirit Today" a booklet I had published in the 1970's when I was teaching a course at what is now Davis College near Binghamton, N.Y.

"And this is the record that God has given to us eternal life, and this life is in his Son. "He that has the Son has life: and he that has not the Son of God has not life" I John 5:11-12.

Good Things Are Always Happening

W hen God is working in a local church made up of His redeemed, regenerated saints, good things are always happening.

Right here we absolutely must understand a vital truth about a local church. Today a local church is two things. It **is** *an organization*, and if it is a Biblical local church, it is *a living organism*.

As an organization, growth is measured in numbers and dollars. This may be from God or just the result of some worldly, secular method of drawing people to the organization. When it is from God, peoples' "lives" are transformed, not merely religious habits (going to church, becoming involved in programs, etc.).

As a living organism, growth is measured in living terms (new life and new attitudes toward sin and God, especially a new love for God and His Word). A sure evidence of life and growth from God is when we see a person whose passion is the *Glory of God*.

I saw a great example of this the night I first heard a sixteen year old girl pray, "Father, help us to love You for Yourself and just want Your good and glory."

I had baptized that young lady several years earlier, and she had been attending all of our Wednesday Bible studies and prayer times ever since that time. Our study for the most part of the past year was "God's Purpose for Himself in Creation and Redemption." We went through all the Scriptures where God tells us who He is and how He brought all things into being out of nothing, all for His Glory. When His perfect creation was desecrated by sin, He had a plan to deal with that sin, by He Himself becoming an offering for sin. Now, we who were the main objects of that fallen creation could be forgiven, reconciled, and again be to the praise of His Glory, His purpose for us from before the foundation of the world. *We could again love Him, because He first loved us,* not merely for the things He could give us.

This young lady got it. She saw the purpose for her existence (to love God and enjoy Him forever). I last talked to that young lady four weeks ago. She still **has it** more than forty years after that night I first heard her pray that prayer.

This is the number one evidence that God is working, unhindered, in an individual. That ones main concern is the *Glory of God,* and that individual knows the work God began in him when he placed his faith in Jesus Christ, He will continue until he is completely transformed into His likeness at His return. *(PHILIPPIANS `1:6; 2:12-16; I JOHN 3:1-3).*

The good things that are always happening when God is working are these everyday evidences flowing from a life of one filled with, and overflowing from, the indwelling Holy Spirit (*JOHN 7:37-39*). His inward life is *one of singing and making melody to the Lord.* He is *always giving thanks for all things, to God His Father,* and he manifests a submissive spirit toward his brothers and sisters in Christ *(EPHESIANS 5:18-21).*

The good things that are always happening when God is working are all of those things mentioned in the book of **Titus.** They are the good works expressed in the lives of those who are constantly *looking for that blessed hope, the glorious return of our Great God and Saviour, Jesus Christ.* They are the good works constantly flowing from one whom Christ gave Himself to *redeem and purify unto Himself (TITUS 2:11-15).*

The good things that are always happening when God is working are the good deeds and attitudes expressed toward one another when each member of the Body of Christ utilizes the gifts, material goods, and talents God has given to each of His own. That is, when they are utilized in love (*I CORINTHIANS 12-14, especially 13:1-3*), and not for self-gratification.

The good things that are always happening when God is working are the good things that transpire in the life of one who understands that his life is not divided. (part sacred and part secular) He knows that his body is the temple of the Holy Spirit, that he was bought with a price, that he does not belong to himself, and that his purpose in life is to glorify God (*I CORINTHIANS 6:14-20*). He knows all he does is to be done *to the glory of God* (*I CORINTHIANS 10:31*). He knows he was created for God's Glory and that he was redeemed for the same purpose. Simply stated, he is one who loves God and finds his joy in pleasing Him.

The good things that are always happening when God is working are the changes that take place in the lives of those who are being *transformed from glory unto glory as they grow in the grace and knowledge of Jesus Christ (II CORINTHIANS 3:16-18; II PETER 3:17-18)*. The desire of their hearts is expressed so well by the hymn writer when he penned these lines:

> *"More like the Master I would ever be*
> *More of His meekness, more humility,*
> *More zeal to labor, more courage to be true,*
> *More consecration for work He bids me do."*

Any co-laborer with God who is a pastor-shepherd as well, will keep the goal God has for His own, ever before His flock (*ROMANS 8:28-30*). He will ever be reminding the flock of which He is their shepherd, that we are on this journey together and that each of us is to be practicing the *"one anothers"* of God's Word, daily, out of faith and love.

The local church, as an organization, consists of individuals who become members by joining upon agreeing with the doctrinal beliefs and practices of that particular church.

The local church, as an organism, consists of those God Himself has called out of the world, through His Word (the Gospel), and made them living members of one another (a living body) of which Christ is the Head (*I CORINTHIANS 12:12-14, 18, 25*, and *27*; *EPHESIANS 4:1-16*).

When a local church is made up of those whom the Holy Spirit has regenerated (imparted Eternal Life) and baptized into Christ's Body (His Church), good will flow from that church as an organization as well as from the church as a living organism.

When a local church, as an organization, takes precedent over the Church as Christ's Body, bad things also happen. The worst of those things is that "church" becomes: **how many attend, what is done, and how it is done when we are gathered together. That simply means church becomes a place where we go for an hour or so each week instead of <u>WHO WE ARE 168 HOURS EACH WEEK.</u>**

When a church operates first and foremost as a living organism (as Christ's Body), the outward evidence of God working will be seen, not primarily in what takes place when His people are gathered together, but what takes place in the lives of each member in the home, in the workplace, at school, and in the community where each lives, and primarily how we interact with and toward our fellow members of Christ's Body, to which we are vitally joined together.

We are members one of another, and the way we treat and minister to one another is the primary way we show, to the unbelieving world around us, that we are Christ's disciples (*JOHN 13:34, 35*).

"Good works" springing out of minds filled with God's Word, and hearts filled with His love are what we will see when God is working . <u>When God is working, good things are always happening.</u>

As a pastor, I did everything I could possibly think of to keep His sheep feeding in the green pastures of His Word. Preaching and teaching from the pulpit, always teaching a Sunday School class, literally conducting dozens of home Bible studies (some lasting a month or so, on a particular subject, and some lasting for years). I gave out many books to read, whose purpose was to teach the Word of God. For years, we, as a church, read the same devotional book daily, on which I commented each Sunday (Devotionals such as "<u>Renewed Day by Day</u>" by A.W. Tozer and "<u>My Utmost for His Highest</u>" by Oswald Chambers). In addition to all of these, there were hundreds of counseling sessions which were, for the most part, instructions from God's Word concerning Biblical principles for living. Knowing the transformation God did in my own life over the years, through His Word, my desire was, and still is, to see Him do the same in others.

One of the greatest paradoxes of our day is that there is such a hunger for the Word of God, while those who hunger fill their minds on the *riches, cares, and pleasures of this life,* seldom even reading, let alone feasting, on the Living Word of God that lays on the stand beside them. A daily diet that includes a generous helping of God's Word would quench that hunger and promote good spiritual health and growth that will be evident in life changes (more like Christ, a concern for others and less for self).

*"All scripture is given by inspiration of God, and is profitable for doctrine, for reproof, for correction, for instruction in righteousness, that the man (and woman) of God may be perfect (mature), thoroughly furnished unto **all good works,"** (II TIMOTHY 3:16, 17).* It is these "Good Works" that comprise **the good things that are always happening when God is working in a local church body**.

Following is an example of what I am trying to say happens in a life when God is working in that individual.

"Pastor, I'm upset with your preaching." Those words did not surprise me coming from her. She was upset by many of the things I did, or in some cases, things I did not do. She was upset because I allowed the youth leaders to make and sell candles at Christmas time. She was also upset when I was a day late getting to the hospital to visit her daughter in law. She was upset when the young people collected thousands of soda and "beer" cans to earn money to go to summer camp. She was upset that I left the parsonage garage doors open. She was really upset when she believed that my family and I had overstayed our vacation.

Returning to the original complaint, my telephone rang. The voice at the other end was insistent, "I need to see you, and I need to see you now!" As I was hanging up the phone, my wife demanded, "What does **that woman** want now?"

I didn't have an answer, but I was about to find out, for in ten minutes I was at her house. As we sat down at her kitchen table, on which laid her open Bible, she burst out, "Pastor, I'm upset with your preaching."

"What bothers you about my preaching?" was my question to her.

"Well, it sounds to me like you are trying to make ministers out of all of us."

"You got it, Arlene! You got it! Praise the Lord!" was my enthusiastic response.

"What do you mean **'I got it'**?" she inquired.

"Just that! That is what I'm trying to do."

"I don't get it. You're our minister. We're not ministers."

"Arlene, the Church is Christ's Body. Each member is connected to the Head and vitally connected to each other. Just as each member of my body cooperates (works together with) every other member of my body as the head directs, so each one of His Body ministers with, to, and for each other, all for the Glory of Him Who is the Head. In His Body, we are all ministers, to use whatever gifts and talents He has given us for His Glory."

As Arlene had her Bible in front of her, we went through the main Scriptures that speak of the Church being Christ's Body (*I CORINTHIANS 12-14; EPHESIANS 4; ROMANS 12*).

After a few minutes of searching and studying, she said, "Why didn't I hear these things before? I don't remember any other pastors teaching this."

"I cannot answer that question, but now that you see it, just start using what God has given you to 'minister' to others for His Glory," was my reply.

Her next comment was, "I don't know any gifts or talents I have. I know I can't teach."

With a big smile, I said, "One of the best meals I have ever eaten was right here at this table. **You can cook**! There is always someone in need of a good meal." We both laughed.

Arlene got it. How do I know **she got it**?

The outward evidence:

1. Instead of complaining about our vacations being too long, each year, the day we left for our vacation, she came by with

a big platter of cookies for us to eat on our way. She even said, "Have a good time."

2. She baked and served the wedding cake at our daughter's Wedding.
3. She reminded our daughter, the next year, to have something Special for our Twenty-fifth Anniversary (another cake).
4. On more than one occasion I was told by Arlene's neighbors, how faithful she was by meeting their need. (She just loved to cook and bake.)
5. Most "*murmurings and disputings*" were gone. (*PHILIPPIANS2:14*).

God had, through His Word, spoken to Arlene, and she was growing up (spiritually). She was now manifesting works that were glorifying to God instead of the old gripes and complaints that grieve His heart and hurt His children.

Another grows up by a changed attitude

"You don't see him teaching a class nor coming prayer meeting, do you?"

I could not believe my ears when I heard those words, especially the Pharisaic tone in which they were spoken, in response to my praise of a man whom I had noticed repairing things around the church and also observed helping several Christians in the church, fixing breakdowns in their homes. The implication was that the exercise of his gift of helps could not possibly be compared with the spiritual work he was doing.

When I tried to explain that he was ministering to Christ's Body with his talents, he became even more indignant. I used the same Scriptures I had used with Arlene just a short time before, but he just could not see it at that time.

Several years passed and one day he came to me and said, "Pastor, God has been dealing with me about my proud attitude." He had read, "*Let nothing be done through strife or vainglory, but in lowliness of mind let each esteem others better than themselves.*

Look not every man on his own things, but every man also on the things of others," *(PHILIPPIANS 2:3-4).*

The man I was praising never knew how that other man felt about his "insignificant" ministry, but praise God, I have seen them both working together in harmony and unity for God's Glory, for many years since those incidents took place. Both continued to minister using the gifts and talents God had given to each of them; one taught and the other continued to fix things. Both continued to grow in grace and knowledge of their Lord Jesus Christ. **Attitude! Attitude! It is all about attitude!**

"Let this mind be in you, which was also in Christ Jesus," **(PHILIPPIANS 2:5).**

What Mind?

"...for I am Meek and lowly in heart..." (MATTHEW 11:29), is His answer.

"...God resists the proud, but gives grace unto the humble." *(JAMES 4:6).*

When God is working, good things are always happening.

Since the good things that are always happening when God is working, and God does His work through His Word by His Spirit, our role is simple. *"Let the Word of God dwell in you richly, in all wisdom spiritual understanding, teaching and admonishing one another, in psalms and hymns and spiritual songs singing with grace in your hearts to the Lord. And whatever you do in word or deed, do all in the name of the Lord Jesus, giving thanks to God and the Father by Him," COLOSSIANS 3:16, 17.*

What are the *"good things"* that will be evident when we let His Word dwell in us and become obedient to His command in verse 17?

1. Wives will submit unto their husbands.

2. Husbands will love their wives and not be bitter toward them.
3. Children will obey their parents.
4. Parents (fathers and mothers) will not provoke their children to anger.
5. Servants (employees) will obey (serve well) their employers in singleness of heart, fearing God.
6. Summed up, *whatever we do, we will do it heartily as unto the Lord, and not unto men, for we know we serve the Lord Christ* 168 hours each week and not merely the local, organized church, 2 or 3 hours each week (*COLOSSIANS 3:18-25*).

When God is working, good things are always happening.

God works through His Word to transform lives, and this transformation is done on the inside (*"Christ in you the hope of Glory."* (*COLOSSIANS 1:27*).

His new covenant is, *"...written, not with ink, but with the Spirit of the living God: not in tables of stone, but in fleshly tables of the heart,"* (*II CORINTHIANS 3:3; HEBREWS 10:16*).

As co-laborers with God, our biggest job is getting the Infallible Word of God from the pages of the Book into the minds and hearts of God's people. To do this in this country, where we have multiple copies of the Word of God in our own language, sounds so simple. All a Bible teaching pastor (shepherd) needs to do is feed the flock a good meal from God's Word on Sunday and tell them to be sure to feed themselves from the Word of God daily (like those in Berea - *ACTS 17:10, 11)*. As they read and study God's Word, to know and obey Him, **good things will happen**. Alas, that is not the way it always works. For the most part, God's Word, which we claim to believe and upon which we base our relationship with God, we let lay on a shelf from one Sunday to the next while we fill our minds with untold hours of this world's problems (news, entertainment, and even some of the filth so prevalent on every hand). Instead of growing to be more like Christ, many of us who claim to be followers of Jesus Christ are becoming more like father Adam. Could it be that there are some of us who are like the people of

EZEKIEL 33:30-33, the foolish man of *MATTHEW 7:26-28*, the Jews in *ROMANS 2:17-29*, especially *verse 29*, or many of those who came out of Egypt with Moses (*I CORINTHIANS 10:1-15 and HEBREWS 4:1-2), or* those in Crete who Paul described to Titus (*TITUS 1:16)*, or the self-deceived that James spoke of in *JAMES 1:22-25?* **I am not judging, just asking a question.**

This last chapter is about **good things that are always happening when God is working.** God can and does do many "good things" through a loving church, as an organization, when its members are faithful in the use of their gifts, talents, and abilities, and as well, their time and money He has, in grace, given to them. Here we are talking about the "good things" that are always happening when God is working in a local church as an organism. They happen just as naturally as each member of my physical body cooperates with every other member, because they are *ONE.* We are talking about (*EPHESIANS 2:10, MATTHEW 5:16 and PHILIPPIANS 2:12-15)* those good works that were done in response to the Head's (Christ's) direction. They are outward manifestations of God's promises believed, His invitations accepted, His commandments obeyed, His warnings heeded, and His instructions followed. They are just some of the "good things" that come **from Him who is working in us** who are not only *hearers of His Word, but doers as well* (*MATTHEW 7:24-29).*

All of the following things I have witnessed, some of them more than once, many of them many times, and I record them here as they come to my mind. They all came to pass over the years I have been a co-laborer with Christ. Notice the simplicity of each incident.

"Where did you get that car?"

"Charlie gave it to me," was the reply.

When Charlie was asked why he gave the car, he said, "God told me to give it to him." *"But whosoever hath this world's good, and seeth his brother have need, and shutteth up his compassions from him, how dwelleth the love of God in him? My little children let us not love in word, neither in tongue, but in deed and in truth." First John 3:16-17*

Charlie gave this simple explanation of that gift in a note, with that Scripture included, to me, to give to the Motor Vehicle Bureau, when they wanted to know why someone would give a car away. It said, "Pastor Walter had no car. We (Charlie and his wife) had two cars, so we gave him one of them. It seems strange that a simple act of love done in the name of Christ would need an explanation" Yes, I was the recipient of Charlie's second car.

When God is working in lives, good things always happen.

"Pastor, we have all the support we need to go to the foreign mission field." Those words were spoken by a young couple from the church who had committed to serve as missionaries on a foreign field.

Surprised, I replied, "I thought you were still $500/ month short."

"We were, but five more people from the church made that up and a little more."

It is good when a local church, as an organization, votes to give support to missions. It is even better to hear God has laid it on the hearts of five individuals to give $500 /month to support a couple from our church family God has called to serve Him on a foreign mission field. **When God is working in lives, good things are always happening.**

It was a Sunday afternoon when our doorbell rang. There stood Jerry, a teenage boy. He said, "Pastor, I want to be baptized. This morning, when you said that all believers should be baptized in obedience to God, I knew I wanted to obey Him."

Less than two hours later, Jim came to my door. We had the same conversation I had just had with Jerry.

Jerry and Jim are just two of a long list of those who came to me with their testimony of their faith in Christ who just wanted to be obedient to Him by being baptized. The first was my mother (who you read about earlier in this book) along with Betty and her daughter, Sue. There was Charlie, Lucille, Dan, Steve, and then Roger and his son Bryan. Then there were many married couples like Mark and Chris, Henry and Lois, Phil and Judy, Gary and Sue, Bob and Joanne, Buster and Pat, and Ted and Irene, just to name a few.

When people come to be baptized, because they say they just want to be obedient to God's Word, you know God is working in them. They understand that baptism is not just a church ritual to be observed, but that it is a public acknowledgment of their faith in Christ and His death, burial, and resurrection on their behalf. **When God is working in lives, good things are always happening.**

"Are you guys keeping warm over there in that cottage?" I asked three boys as I picked them up for our Saturday morning boys' basketball game. They, with their mother, were living in a summer cottage on a lake that was frozen solid. I knew there wasn't any insulation in any of those cottages.

"Yeah, we're keeping warm. Mr. M. keeps our fuel oil barrel filled, and he brings us things to eat, too," they answered.

This was not an isolated incident with Mr. M. Over the years I had three other people in the church tell me how Mr. M. had helped them during difficult times. In each of these situations, Mr. M. could have gone to the deacon's board and asked for help on their behalf, which would have been a good thing, but instead, he took seriously, the words of Paul to the churches of Galatia, *"As we have, therefore, opportunity, let us do good unto all people, "especially" unto them who are of the household of faith," (GALATIANS 6:10).*

In *I TIMOTHY 6:17-21,* Paul closes the letter to young pastor Timothy, with a charge he is to give to those with material wealth. He says, *"Charge them… to do good, that they be rich in good works, ready to distribute, willing to communicate (share their wealth with others)."*

When the Mr. M.'s in a church body hear God speak these words, good things always happen.

"If it were not for M and J (a Christian couple) sticking by us and reminding us of what God says about marriage and the home, we would never have made it."

You will never know the joy that comes when a pastor hears words like those. I have had people, many times over the years, come to tell me of a couple who needed help with their marriage, but few who felt they were capable of doing what M and J did. I am sure there are more who could, if they would. At least Paul believed there were many among the saints in Rome when he wrote, *"I myself am persuaded of you, my brethren, that you also are full of goodness, filled with all knowledge, "able also to admonish (competent to gently correct) one another," (ROMANS 15:14).*

Most times all God needs is someone who is available and genuinely cares (loves with His love) to do what M and J did. **When God is working, good things always happen.**

"Pastor, I don't know how you are going to take what I am going to say, but my wife and I are going to go to the mission field."

Ordinarily, I, as any co-laborer with God, would have jumped with glee at such an announcement. Any time God calls a young couple to serve Him in what we call full-time service," it is a time of rejoicing, but this time it was a little bit different.

I quickly responded, "Dan, you have just made me the most happy and yet sad man, all at the same time." The explanation of that statement is simple. Dan and Peggy had grown up in the church. Dan had gone through the Bible Institute I had graduated from many, many years before. Peggy was a Registered Nurse. They had pastored a small country church for several years. Then our church had called him to be my assistant, where he had served admirably. My thought was that he would become the senior pastor when it came time for me to leave, but with that statement, all of my plans for Dan's future were out the window.

It's probably best I do not try to plan others' futures. That is best left up to them and God.

Twenty years later, when asked to comment on my first book, "Fifty Years a Country Pastor," Dan responded by saying, "Fifty Years a Country Pastor presents the ministry as it is: real people, real problems, and a real shepherd with a heart to serve and please the One and only Master Shepherd. Having grown up under the tutelage of this author, I was personally mentored and impacted by the Biblical principles taught to me in person and now in print. Now serving as a career missionary in South America, it was refreshing to read this book and be reminded of what I was exposed to some twenty plus years ago.

"Here is a book that should be read by all members of rural and small town churches. It is not about building mega churches out of small town and rural assemblies. It's about a pastor-teacher, called of God to be one with Him in building lives for His Glory. My wife and I are here in Paraguay, doing the same thing, greatly as a result of growing up under this Author's ministry."

Dan and his wife are just two of a number of people from that church whom God has called to serve Him full-time, both here and on foreign fields. **<u>When God is working, good things always happen.</u>**

"I'm just doing what I promised God I would do, back there on our wedding day so many years ago." Those were the words of a man who day after day and night after night, for several years, took care of his bed-ridden wife, along with all that entailed.

"For better, for worse, for richer, for poorer, in sickness and in health, 'til death us do part;" he believed those words were truly vows made before God and that God would give him the love, patience and stamina to fulfill them for her welfare and God's Glory.

When he said that, I thought of several others who did the same for their mates, but most of all, my mind went back to when I was seven years old. That was when we moved in with Grandpa and Grandma, because they were no longer able to take care of themselves (my mother's parents). I have already spoken of my father's parents earlier in this book, in an entirely different light. Grandma was no longer able to lie down and Grandpa had what is today called dementia or Alzheimer's Disease, to the point where he no longer knew anyone and was not able to even dress himself. He never became mean, like some others I have seen. He just became child-like again. My brother and I liked that, because he was one of us, but to Mom and Dad, he was more than a hand full.

Grandma died a year after we moved in. She fell over dead as she was threading a needle to sew on a button. My mother caught her in her arms and gently lowered her to the floor as she took her last breath.

With Grandpa, it was a much different situation. Day after day, for more than two years, while Dad was at work, Mom had the tremendous responsibility of caring for her father; Time after time I saw her do the impossible with Grandpa. The day he wandered off into the woods above our home is the incident I remember the most. Try as she might, Mom could not find him anywhere. She called and called and searched everywhere she could think of. Then she heard a faint sound from the woods, calling, "Help! I need help!"

I ran along with Mom into the edge of the woods. There, beside a big maple tree, lay Grandpa. What a mess! He evidentially had to go to the bathroom and had gotten his pants part way off and tried to lean against that maple tree while he relieved himself. Then he fell, and trying to get up, was covered from head to toe, in his own feces.

When Mom saw the mess, she began to cry and say, over and over as she helped him to his feet, "O Dad! O Dad! O Dad!"

Helping him get those messed up clothes off, she led him to the house, continuing to cry and say, "Oh Dad! Oh Dad!" To this day, I do not know if she was primarily speaking to Grandpa or crying out to her Heavenly Daddy for strength to endure such situations. I do know she spent the next hour cleaning Grandpa and dressing him in clean clothes. She then went to her room to clean herself, and more importantly, to spend more time crying and talking to her Lord Jesus, where she found the strength she needed to face the next trial with Grandpa, or maybe one caused by my younger brother or me.

Grandpa smiled throughout the whole ordeal and then said, "Thank you Cora." (Cora was a girlfriend he had dated before he and Grandma were married, but that was the name he called Mom until the day he died. His mind just kept getting worse.)

Why did I go into such detail about my mother's ministry (that is the way she accepted it) God had given her in taking care of Grandpa? The answer is because I was there and saw these things first hand. I am sure the details were similar with Grover, B and D, M and L, and so many more I could name.

What was God doing in and for each of these people? As the hymn says, "He granted more grace as the burdens grew greater." As they believed and obeyed (*HEBREWS 4:14-16*), God was working in their lives. They were growing in His Grace and becoming more like Him. **When God is working, good things are always happening,** even in what often seems like the worst of times.

If God is working in the rest of us in a local church family of His children, what will we be doing while those of His children are going through "tribulations" such as those we have just described, plus a hundred others that our Lord promised us would come while we are in this world (*JOHN 16:33*)?

I could only hope we would be doing what we promised in song every time a new member was extended the "the right hand of fellowship." Hear them once again:

"Blest be the tie that binds, our hearts in Christian love,
The fellowship of kindred minds is like to that above."
Before our Father's throne, we pour our ardent prayers
Our fears, our hopes, our aims are one, our comforts, and our cares.
We share our mutual woes, our mutual burdens bear,
And often for each other flows the sympathizing tear."

Could it be that an awful lot of us only see a local church as an organization of religious people who show our religion by subscribing to a set of doctrinal beliefs and being faithful by going through our Sunday ritual? Maybe we even sing that song as a part of that ritual? Could it be also, that "the tie that binds" us together is just words on paper and not the Lord Jesus Christ living in each of us? I leave that for each of us to answer for him or her self.

What I do know for sure is that **when God is working in any one of us, good things will always happen.** I have been on both ends of the "good things" God does in a life where His Spirit dwells unquenched; sometimes on the receiving end and sometimes on the giving end, and thus it should be. In either case, it is God that does the work. *"To Him be the Glory!"*

God is busy fixing things, and when His fixing (sanctifying) process is unhindered in any life, **good things will always happen.**

There is not room here to recount all the times where I, as God's under shepherd and co-worker, have been the recipient of good things. Each time I have to learn the same lesson God has taught me so many times before. That is: when those Dennises, Walters, Rinkers, Holdens, Franks, Kens, Fletchers, Alberts, Mikes, Harmons, Garys, Roberts, Jerrys, Harrys, Bobs, Philips, Thomases, Floyds, Johns, Pitchers, Charlies, and so many more to numerous to mention offer help, in whatever form, to graciously accept it as from the Lord with a humble "Thank You."

The other side that is absolutely necessary on my part is given in Galatians 6:10. "As we (I) have therefore opportunity, let us (me) do good unto all men, especially unto them who are of the household of faith." This is all part of a local church operating as a body. Those who see God's local church only as an organization never experience the blessings that are a continual experience in the lives of those who see themselves as living members of Christ's Body and therefore <u>vitally</u> connected to one another with a concern for each other (*1 COR. 12:25-27*). All those "cups of cold water" and "five loaves and two small fish" given in Jesus' name are what we are talking about.

Giving to under supported country pastors is nothing new. As a child my parents had no money but we did have chickens. In those early years I helped catch more than one chicken for our "poor pastor." The opportunities for the "poor country pastor" to do good things for members of the flock his Heavenly Shepherd has entrusted to his care are never ending, every thing from milking cows and delivering a calf to all those untold hours spent rescuing His straying sheep from the devils snares. As one of His co-workers I have been one with Him in doing these and a hundred other things few of the flock ever know about unless they are the ones involved. **WHEN GOD IS WORKING GOOD THINGS ARE ALWAYS HAPPENING.**

APPENDIX

The appendix to this book is taken from a booklet I had published thirty years ago. They were originally sermons I had preached from the pulpits of the last two churches I had pastored. They were a part of the curriculum those years I taught at what is now Davis College near Binghamton, N.Y.

It was at the continuous prodding of David Holden who was a member of the church I was then pastoring that finally convinced me to write the booklet. He was the manager of a small Christian Press who had told me many times how these sermons (Bible Studies) entitled "Your Questions Answered" had affected his life.

Over the years many have told me of the effect they have had upon their lives. During the past year 2009 (thirty years after the fact) four of the students I had in those classes at what is now Davis College have let me know personally the effect they had in their lives and ministries down through the years. Dan, a career missionary to Paraguay, Gary, a career missionary to Peru, Pat, a Christian Camp director ever since graduating from Davis College, and Walt, a professor at Davis College.

Then there are the words of David Holden, who is now with the Lord which he wrote in the Publisher's forward to the booklet. "One of the greatest blessings of my life has been to sit under the ministry of Rev. James Walter. (He was my pastor for a number of years, and I rejoice at each opportunity to hear the Word from his lips.) My soul has been greatly blessed in hearing a number of these messages delivered from his own pulpit, and now to see them being placed into permanent form thrills my heart…Here, beyond dispute, are the answers to vital questions regarding the 'experiencing' of the ministry of the Holy Spirit in this present day. The answers are all in the Book. (The Bible)"

Four of those chapters (questions) make up the appendix of this book.

24 QUESTIONS...

Experiencing
the Work of
THE HOLY SPIRIT
Today

by
REV. JAMES A. WALTER
Pastor
SOUTH APALACHIN BAPTIST CHURCH
Apalachin NY
Teacher
PRACTICAL BIBLE TRAINING SCHOOL
Bible School Park, NY
MIRACLE MANOR
Spencer, NY
1978
Published by
BIBLE LIGHTHOUSE PRESS
SAYRE, PENNA. 18840

INTRODUCTION

T HE HOLY SPIRIT, Who is the Author of the Scriptures, is the One Who lives in the Believer. The Truth He caused to be written in a Book, He wishes to manifest in lives today. To be sure there is much today that is called "The Holy Spirit's work" which is contrary to those things He caused to be written. This can never be His Work, as He, being God, cannot contradict Himself. Then, too, there is much truth that is entirely objective. All Truth in this category must simply be accepted by faith with no present experience involved, except the peace and joy that results in believing God. Thus, a simple principle that always must be observed is that we are willing to test any and all our experiences with the Written Revelation, the Verbally Inspired Word of God.

Creatures of Extremes

Another observation that I have seen for many years is that we are creatures of extremes. In two major ways we, who are Christians, tend to manifest this. First, we tend to emphasize the doctrinal aspect of Christianity almost to the exclusion of the experiential or the other way around. The theme of the Doctrinal Christian (Church) is "Thus saith the Lord" while the theme of the experiential Christian (Church) is "Let me tell you what God is doing," In this book we endeavor to bring these two into balance.

Secondly, being creatures of extremes we tend to live either in the past or the future. Unbelievers either talk about "The good old days" or build "air castles" in the future. We, as Christians, are a lot the same way when it comes to God's working. We talk about the wonderful ways in which He has worked in the past or the tremendous things He shall do in the future. There is nothing wrong with this except we live today, not yesterday, nor tomorrow. What about the "NOW"? The past is "memories" and the future is "hope," both of them blessed for the one who walks with God in the "Now," but a mixture of blessedness and despair for the one who lives in them. You see the one who must reach either into the past or future to find God at work is an empty person. He talks about the "Great things God hath done" or the wonderful blessings that shall be "when we all get to Heaven." If you ask him for a current testimony of God's work in his life, he remains silent; he is unaware of any. He knows little or nothing of the experience of the song writer who wrote "All The Way My Saviour Leads Me." No, it is the Christian who is living in the "Now" that is experiencing a fulfilled life. He knows God has done great things yesterday and will do wonderful things tomorrow, but the most wonderful thing to him is God's "working in him" today.

To Be Aware of God's Working Today

Although we are thankful for a revelation of God's past activities and rejoice in His promises for the future, the purpose of this book is to make us aware of what He wants to do FOR, IN, and THROUGH us today. Then, too, each one of us may have some wonderful past experiences with God and anticipate many more in the future, but in this book we will primarily concern ourselves with the present aspect of God, The Holy Spirit's Work. And, in much of His present work, He desires to involve us. May He, through the reading of this book, create in you a desire to "Experience His Work Today".

Purpose of This Book

Allow me to add just one more note about this book. This author has read literally dozens of books on the subject of the Holy Spirit over the past twenty years. Most have been helpful in some respect, but many have also had what this author considers a glaring weakness. That is, they have been reactionary rather than revelatory. By this I mean one can detect the author's desire to defend his position as opposed to another's. Also, one gets the feeling that unless you accept his position exactly, there is no possibility that you could be experiencing a work of God in your life. In so far as it is possible, this book is free of this reactionary spirit. It is this author's desire that this book be revelatory, that it might be used by The Holy Spirit to bring its readers into a right relationship and fellowship with the Blessed Triune God.

QUESTION ONE:

Religion or God at Work -Which?
PHILIPPIANS 2:13 For it is God that worketh in you...

THIS SHORT PASSAGE from God's Word expresses the major difference between the Christianity of the Bible and the religions of the world. Christianity is God's work; the religions of the world are but a poor substitute for that which God has done in the past, is now doing, and shall bring to a culmination in the future. Although this book will deal primarily with that which God is doing today, we must for a few moments look into the past and then to the future. We look back to see the purpose He had in His heart from eternity and also to see how He provided all the requisites to carry out that purpose. We look to the future to see that purpose a reality fulfilled. Of course, to look into eternity past or future we need Revelation. Apart from a clear understanding of that which He purposed in the past and an unshakable faith in that which He purposed He will perform, we cannot possibly understand what He is doing today. The Bible alone is the only infallible revelation of God's acts (past, present or future).

The Bible reveals God the Father as the originator of an Eternal Purpose in full cooperation with His Son and Spirit. The Bible reveals God the Son as the Central Figure in that purpose working in full co-operation with His Father and The Holy Spirit. The Bible reveals God The Spirit transforming that purpose into reality in full co-operation with The Father and The Son.

The Primary Work of the God-Head

The Father's primary work was a work done in eternity before the world or man was. It was there the plans were made for creation. It was there the thought of children in His own likeness originated. It was there the Church was purposed. It was there the Son agreed to become the Lamb slain for the sins of the world.

The Son's primary work was done in history past. By entering the human race supernaturally through the Virgin Birth, He was able to deal with the one major obstacle that would hinder the fulfillment of the Father's purpose. That is SIN. By His death on Calvary's Cross He defeated him that had the power of death (the Devil). By His death He made reconciliation with God in behalf of fallen, sinful man. By His Resurrection He made eternal life available to man.

The Holy Spirit's primary work is accomplished in the hearts and lives of people today. In full accord with the Father's plans and the Son's provision The Spirit today is at work. It is His working that distinguishes Biblical Christianity from all religion.

The Culmination of the Work of The Trinity

Now, before we look at the differences between God's working and man's religion, let's look into the future and see the culmination of the Trinity's Work.

In the last two chapters of our Bible we have revealed not only an Eternal God with an eternal purpose, but The Eternal Trinity with a purpose fulfilled. The Father's purpose of creation (a holy, pure creation) is now a reality. The Son made this possible by dealing with sin at the cross. The Spirit Who brooded over a fallen creation in the first chapters of our Bibles is rejoicing with the Church He has formed of those chosen of the Father and Redeemed by the Son.

Throughout eternity this must abide for the Eternal God can do only eternal work. Apart from this revelation of the future we could never see this. For to look at the creation today and to look at men today (even the best of them) we surely cannot see eternal perfection nor anything near it. But as sure as the Father purposed it and as sure as the Son died and rose again to make it possible, The Spirit is at work today to bring it to pass. It is His work that we shall look at and compare with the world's religions.

Similarity of Some Aspects

There are many aspects of God's work and the world's religions that on the surface look much alike. For this reason many are easily deceived into accepting one of the religions and believing it is of God. For instance, all religions respect prayer. One of the manifestations of God at work in an individual is that he becomes a man of prayer. Outwardly the two may look very much the same. Throughout the remainder of this chapter when we use the word *RELIGION* we mean Christianity as a whole in one or more of its many expressions. These expressions of religion always contain four outward manifestations. They are "Rites, Rituals, Rules, and Regulations." The outward manifestations of The Spirit of God's work in an individual may look much like these same four R's. It is for this reason that it is not always easy to distinguish between one who is practicing a religion and one in whom The Holy Spirit is at work. The one who merely practices a religion by an observance of certain rites, rituals, rules, and regulations, knows nothing of God's work within him in an experiential way. The one providing the energy and power is that man himself and not God. His purpose for such a practice is usually one of two things. He is either trying to satisfy that inward desire for peace and satisfaction (which can only be permanently satisfied by God Himself) or he is doing what he feels is his duty toward God and his fellow man.

Examining the Four "R's"

The one in whom God is working will also show forth outward expressions. But, his outward expression will be the results of something that is taking place within. He will be *"working out his salvation"* that The Spirit of God is working within him. As we have said, when all we see and know is the outward, the two may look identical.

Let us see if we cannot take these four R's of religion and see what each one would be to one in whom God is at work, but again, there is a great difference between the two. The religionist *says prayers* while the one in whom God is at work *prays*. I often wonder how much of our praying at mealtime and devotional time is ritual and how much is genuine expression of thankfulness and fellowship with God. (In a later chapter we shall deal in much greater detail with The Holy Spirit and prayer.)

Singing has always formed a large part of Christian worship. As a pastor who has looked out over congregations hundreds of times while the hymns of praise, thanksgiving, and worship were being sung, I am sure I have seen many observing a ritual rather than worshipping God in Spirit and in Truth. Religion sings words and music while the one in whom God is at work expresses praise, adoration and worship to God through music. I have heard some excellent singers whose talents I have admired greatly but their singing left me empty as it was clear that their singing was merely a performance and an expression of their talents. On the other hand, I have heard some poor singers who moved me greatly as their singing was an expression of genuine praise and worship to God from the Holy Spirit within them. Although we may not always be able to determine the difference, one thing is certain: God knows when singing is a ritual and when it is an expression of the heart in which He dwells.

Another aspect of Christian worship is the reading of The Scriptures. To the one who only has a religion this is just another part of his ritual. He does it because it's customary at certain times during the service. I am sure there are even those who have a daily devotional time when the reading of the Scriptures is merely ritual.

To the one in whom God is at work the reading of the Scriptures is a time of listening to God. He knows that it was through The Scriptures he first heard God speak, and asked entrance into his life, and so each time he hears the Scriptures he continues to listen to see what God has to say to him.

We could go on and on with the many aspects of Christian worship which to the one with only religion are just more rituals to be observed out of custom or habit, but to the one in whom The Holy Spirit is at work are times of precious fellowship and communion with God.

"Rules"

The third major aspect of the one who only has religion is the keeping of rules. Along with his rites and rituals he observes are rules to help govern his conduct and establish some sort of standard for righteousness in his life. Probably the most religious people who ever lived were the Pharisees of Christ's day. They were the rule quoters of all time. I say *QUOTERS* rather than *KEEPERS* because they *"said but did not,"* according to our Lord's judgment of them. They had taken the Old Testament commandments and added centuries of tradition to their book of rules. The Saviour's main accusation against them was that their religion was outward. By the observance of their rites, rituals, rules and regulations they *"appeared righteous before men"* while inwardly they were unchanged and corrupt. The righteousness produced by these observances was obnoxious to God and extremely distasteful to the people who knew them well, for they clearly recognized by their attitudes, deeds and actions that what was in their hearts and what they professed were two completely different things.

To control people by rules is the oldest fault recorded in the Bible of the Church. Several books (GALATIANS and COLOSSIANS) were written primarily to correct this grave error. History is filled with illustrations of man's attempts to control his conduct by adding more rules, and with each attempt there is recorded a subsequent failure. Even today many feel this is the way to change man's conduct. It can never work either for religion or government. The principle taught throughout the Scripture is *"First make the inside clean"* and the outside will take care of itself. Righteous conduct must be the result of a righteous character within, not the result of the outward keeping of rules.

The word *RELIGION* itself comes from the Latin word *"religio"* which means "to restrain or bind." This is exactly what rules do. Religion binds by asking a person to conduct himself contrary to that which he is inside. I cannot begin to count the many professing Christians I have talked with through the years who were miserable because inside they desired to do things the rules of their religion forbade them to do. They were being restrained against their wills by rules of their religion and therefore the pressures within mounted. I have known of several occasions where psychiatrists recommended a change of religion where the rules were not strict, to relieve the inward tensions caused by trying to live by these rules and failing, thus producing extreme guilt feelings.

About here the question always arises: "Doesn't the Christian have rules to follow? Has not God in His Word given certain definite rules the Christian is to keep?" The answer to these questions is so simple that it is often completely overlooked. The one in whom God is working does not see the commands of God's Word as "rules to bind him," but rather as "instructions from a loving Father" to set him free. As we said, the righteous conduct expressed in the true Christian's life is not a result of rule keeping but rather the result of the controlling of the indwelling Holy Spirit. The Apostle Paul puts it this way:

ROMANS 8:2 . . . the law of the Spirit of life in Christ Jesus hath made me free from the law of sin and death.

3 For what the law could not do, in that it was weak through the flesh, God sending his own Son in the likeness of sinful flesh, and for sin, condemned sin in the flesh:

4 That the righteousness of the law might be fulfilled IN US, who walk not after the flesh, but after the Spirit.

The key words are *"in us."* The righteousness of God's commands must be first wrought in us by the indwelling Spirit before it can be expressed in our conduct. If it is not, we are merely expressing the same self—righteousness manifested by the religious-rule keepers.

At Mt. Sinai, God literally wrote ten commandments on tablets of stone. Today, God's Spirit is still writing. His writing today is not a new revelation, but merely his Inspired Word being written inside men by the same Holy Spirit who caused it to be written through men in the first place.

II CORINTHIANS 3.3 Forasmuch as ye are manifestly declared to be the epistle of Christ ministered by us, written not with ink, but with the Spirit of the living God; not in tablet of stone, but IN FLESHLY TABLETS OF THE HEART.

HEBREWS 10.15 Whereof the Holy Ghost also is a witness to us; for after that he had said before,

16 This is the covenant that I will make with them after those days, saith the Lord, I will put my laws into their hearts, and IN THEIR MINDS WILL I WRITE THEM.

"Regulations"

Now let us look at the last of Religion's four R's. That is regulations. While religion's rules establish a standard of righteousness and to a degree help control conduct, regulations help to establish limits and let a person know just how far he can go in any direction. A good illustration of this today is the rating system some religions have of movies. Instead of the old rule many religions used to have: "Thou shalt not attend the theatre," there are now regulations which set limits as to which movies are tolerable for which age bracket. The list of areas where regulations are applied is almost endless. With the increase of things to do and places to go brought about by modem inventions, has come the increase in regulations by religions. And I am sure I do not need to tell you the great frustration, and in many cases the downright rebellion, this has produced among the younger generation. They seem to be able to clearly see the double standards these restrictions have produced in the lives of their proclaimers.

The one in whom *"God is working both to will and do of His good pleasure"* does not have his limits set by outward regulation. The question in his heart is not, "How far can I go in this or that area?" but rather, "Father, what is pleasing unto you?" Then the conclusion he comes to in answer to his question in any given situation is not an out ward regulation, but rather the will of his Father. And that is just where he finds his deepest satisfaction, in doing the will of his heavenly Father. Also, right here we must again say, the Bible is the final and absolute source of the revealed will of God. The answer in any situation must ultimately be in full accord with God's Written Revelation, interpreted to our hearts by His indwelling Holy Spirit.

By this time each of us should be ready to answer the question which is the title of this chapter, "Religion or God at Work - Which?" If you discover that all you have is a religion of rites, rituals, rules, and regulations, this book is not for you, as it is all written for the one in whom God is at work. Of course, if you are willing by faith to turn from all your self-righteousness and sin and cast yourself fully upon Him, He will come in and begin a work in you this very moment. And this work He begins in you is a continuous work that, you can be confident, He will not rest until it is finished.

PHILIPPIANS 1:6 Being confident of this very thing, that He who hath begun a good work in you will perform it until the day of Jesus Christ:

QUESTION TWO:

What is God Doing Today? And Where? and How?

II CORINTHIANS 3:18 But we all, with open face beholding as in a glass the glory of the Lord, are changed into the same image from glory to glory, even as by the Spirit of the Lord.

ONE thing is certain and that is that all being done in the name of the Lord today is not being done by the Lord. In the last chapter we asked the question *"Religion or God at Work—Which ?"* This was to establish the fact that there is a vast difference between religion and God's Work. Although there are many differences between the two, the major difference lies in the sphere in which each operates. Religion is external and seeks to change man from the outside. Being external it deals primarily with CONDUCT while God's work is done within man and deals primarily with CHARACTER.

While our Lord was here upon this earth, he constantly affirmed the principle *"From within out of the heart are the issues of life."* Of course, this philosophy is diametrically opposed to most modern day teaching. The basic idea today is that circumstances and environment cause man to be what he is. Therefore, let us spend our time and energies improving the outside, and the inside will become better. All history only goes to disprove this philosophy. The more improvements man makes in his environment (that are not direct results of a change within him first) the more selfish he becomes. Never before in the history of the world has a more perfect environment (materialistically speaking) existed than exists in the United States today, and never before has there been more selfishness manifested. And most religions (including much of Christianity) has accepted this same philosophy, if not in doctrine at least in practice. Where is God in all this? How much of this is His Work? Much of it is done in His Name but how much is done by Him?

God Continues His Work

Now comes our question: *"What is God doing today?"* According to the Word of God (The Bible) He is still doing what He has been doing for the past 1900 years. He is calling out a people for His Name. The word "church" simply means "called out" From among mankind He is calling a people in. whom He can live and through whom He can reveal Himself. Many things have troubled me through the years, but none so much as the fact that most of those who claim to be *"His called out ones"* do not reveal Him, but continue to reveal selfish old Adam.

The method God has determined to use in calling people to Himself is an extremely simple one. Notice we said *"God is doing this."* That Is God the Holy Spirit. If I am to experience His work in this area, I must be in full co-operation with Him and in utter dependence upon Him. The Apostle Paul said concerning Apollos and himself that they were

I CORINTHIANS 3:9 ... labourers together with God:...

Literally he was saying we are God's fellow workers. He was repeating a truth his Lord spoke while He was on earth when He said

JOHN 5:17 ...My Father worketh hitherto, and I work.
19...The Son can do nothing of himself, but what he seeth the Father do:...

As our Lord Jesus Christ never acted independently of His Father, we cannot act independently of The Holy Spirit and experience the co-operation with Him in calling out a people for His Name. Surely we have employed and are continuing to employ all kinds of methods and means that He will have no part of, in trying to *"get people saved."* The last invitation of the Bible expresses this co-operation with The Holy Spirit in God's work today very beautifully. We read:

REVELATION 22:17 And the Spirit and the bride say, Come. And let him that heareth say, Come. And let him that is athirst come. And whosoever will, let him take the water of life freely.

God Works Through His Word

Throughout this book we will be emphasizing the importance of the written Revelation (The Bible) in doing God's Work, and we will include one chapter exclusively to this subject, but here let me just make one strong statement concerning God's Word. That is,

The Holy Spirit always works in full accord with His Word and nearly always directly through His Word.

The one sure test of determining whether a work is of God or not is simply: Is it in full accord with the Word of God? The Holy Spirit cannot contradict Himself by saying one thing in His Word and doing something opposite in practice. Just one word of caution: Let us make sure we understand there can be a difference between what any one of us may interpret the Bible as teaching on a given subject and what The Holy Spirit actually said on that subject. He does not work according to any one person's (or any one group's) interpretation of His Word, but rather in full accord with what He actually said in His Word.

Salvation —God's Main Business

Someone always asks: *"Isn't it so that God's main business today is salvation?"* To that question we must answer an emphatic "yes." But we must understand the term "salvation." Let us give a definition of salvation that is in full accord with the Scriptures, not a partial definition or even one that does not find its basis in. the Word of God.

SALVATION is the process whereby God takes a. self-centered sinner in the likeness of Adam and transforms him into a God-centered saint in tie likeness of His Son Jesus Christ. Actually, this is The Holy Spirit's Work in Salvation made possible by our Saviour's Work at Calvary in full accord with the Father's eternal plans. Salvation changes people. And that change takes place inside with outward manifestations.

God's Salvation insofar as it concerns man's experience is in three stages. The first is an instantaneous birth; the second a continuous growth, and the third an instantaneous transformation. The first two take place in this life, the third when Christ returns for those in whom The Holy Spirit has accomplished the first two. The first one deals primarily with the spirit of man, the second with the soul of man, and the third with the body of man. The first two take place inside man, the third affecting the whole man (spirit, soul and body).

One of the major problems The Holy Spirit faces in accomplishing His Work of Salvation today is getting us to be one with Him in what He wants to do. We must surely grieve Him and many times quench Him, making it impossible for Him to accomplish what He would like in people's lives. Because we don't know what He is doing, or because we don't know how He does His Work we often become a hindrance rather than a co-laborer together with Him.

God Working In Us

Throughout the remainder of this chapter let each of us think of himself as one in whom the Holy Spirit is at work *"both to will and do of His good pleasure,"* instead of one through whom He is working to reach others. In other words let each of us look at himself as one whom He has *"called out"* of the world for His Name. In another chapter we will deal with His Work done THROUGH US but in this chapter with His Work done IN US.

In order for a Christian to know what The Holy Spirit is doing inside him he must understand the goal God has in mind for all Christians, as all he is doing in us now is moving toward that goal. Here is one of the major differences between God's work and man's work. God is a God with a purpose and a goal toward which He constantly works. Man tends to go in circles, even repeating known mistakes over and over again. The only way any one of us can get out of these vicious cycles is to discover God's purpose for us and then submit to that purpose rather than just drifting with the tide of this world system. Again the only way we can discover what God is doing is through Revelation.

A major passage in God's Word that explains His purpose is

ROMANS 8:28 And we know that all things work together for good to them that love God, to them who are the called according to His PURPOSE,

29 For whom He did foreknow, He also did predestinate to be conformed to the image of His Son, that He might be the firstborn among many brethren.

30 Moreover whom He did predestinate, them He also called: and whom He called, them He also justified: and whom He justified, them He also glorified.

God's ultimate goal for his children then is glorification or to conform them into the likeness of His only begotten Son Jesus Christ All his work in Eternity past (Foreknowledge arid Predestination) as well as his present work (calling and justification) move toward His ultimate work (Glorification). There is no question, but that our ultimate glorification will take place in a moment. We read,

I JOHN 3:2...now are we the sons of God, and it doth not yet appear what we shall be: but we know that WHEN HE SHALL APPEAR, we shall be like him; for We shall see him as he is.

Toward that great event we should all be looking. His appearance for His own is that "blessed hope" that gives God the opportunity to do a present work in anyone who is constantly looking forward to its fulfillment.

Beginning a Continuous Work

His present work then is calling out a people for His name, declaring them righteous on the basis of Christ's work at Calvary and then starting them on their way to glorification or likeness of Christ. This present aspect of God's work is carried on by The Holy Spirit. It becomes an experience inside anyone when they hear his voice through The Word and by faith respond positively to that voice. Inside that one the Holy Spirit performs a birth. Our Saviour called it "Being born of the Spirit." Literally what takes place is a union of God's Spirit and our spirit, making them one.

I CORINTHIANS 6:17 He that is joined unto the Lord is one spirit.

This is the first aspect of our ultimate glorification which is the *"likeness of Christ."* And sad to say, this is the only aspect of the Holy Spirit's present work that many know anything of in their experience. In reality this is just the beginning of a continuous work concerning which The Holy Spirit will not rest until He has completed it in any individual who is trusting Christ as his personal Saviour and Lord.

Moving Toward the Goal

Right here is where we want to take a look at the passage quoted at the beginning of this chapter from II COR. 3. The new birth produces a tremendous change in an individual, but it is just the beginning of many changes that are to be taking place continually in the one in whom The Holy Spirit now dwells. That is what this passage is teaching. *"From glory to glory"* (v. 18) describes the direction the indwelling Holy Spirit takes the believer toward the goal (the image of the Lord).

"The Glory of God" is a most interesting expression in the Scriptures. It is that for which we were created in the beginning (ISAIAH 43:7). It is that which we all came short of (ROMANS 3:23). It is that which was manifested in Jesus Christ (JOHN 1:14). It is that which He gave to His disciples to make them one (JOHN 17:22). It is that to which we are instructed to do all things (I CORINTHIANS 10:31). It is that to which we are called (II PETER 1:3). And it is that to which He intends to bring all His children to share with Him (HEBREWS 2:10).

ROMANS 8:30...For whom he justified, them he also glorified.

The new birth is the first of many aspects of our glorification. In the Scriptures this act of the Holy Spirit is called regeneration or quickening. It simply means the impartation of new life. That is life from above or God's life. In this life is Gods nature. From this nature He desires to manifest His character through us, not by the keeping of external laws, but by the vital process of living His life in us. Again let us emphasize that God's work today is done INSIDE people. He is changing people from the INSIDE. A gospel that only changes man's destiny without changing his character is foreign to God's Word. Yes, any gospel that tells a man he can have his destiny changed without his character being changed is false teaching. In the life of one in whom God has entered and imparted His own life will come a series of changes from that moment until he is presented faultless before God's throne at the Rapture. Each of these gradual changes brings us nearer to the goal (the likeness of Christ).

Therefore, the Holy Spirit's work today is to change those who own Jesus Christ as their Lord and Saviour into His likeness. He begins this with the New Birth and concludes it with our ultimate glorification at the return of Christ. Now He is taking us through a growth *"from glory unto glory"*. If anyone does not discover this to be his experience, I would strongly suggest immediate obedience to the Holy Spirit's admonition in

II CORINTHIANS 13:5 Examine yourself, whether ye be in the faith; prove your own selves. Know ye not your own selves, how that Jesus Christ is in you, except ye be reprobates?

How Is God Working Today?

So far in this chapter we have answered the first two parts of our three part question which form its title. What is God doing today? He is calling out a people for His Name and conforming them into the likeness of His Son. Where is He doing this? In the hearts and minds of those who submit to Him when they hear the Gospel. Now the third aspect of our question: *HOW IS HE DOING THIS?* In our initial passage we read,

II CORINTHIANS 3:18 But we all, with open face beholding as in a glass the glory of the Lord, are changed into the same image...

The glass or mirror from which we see the Glory of Christ reflected is the Word of God. The main purpose of the Bible ever being written was to reveal Him. Our main purpose for reading and studying it should be to know Him as He reveals Himself. As we said, the Holy Spirit works through His Word. He changes people through His Word. As we see our Lord reflected from the pages of God's Word, the Holy Spirit changes us into that same likeness, from one glory unto another.

There is a lot of talk today about experiencing the work of the Holy Spirit. I for one agree that it is needed above all else. But make it clear once again, The Holy Spirit works in full accord with His Word and nearly always directly through His Word. What is really needed is more of us to open the Word of God to see Him as He is, all the time desiring the Holy Spirit to make us like Him.

Let me close this chapter with an illustration I read some years ago. It concerns a Chinaman who came to this country to go to college. After he was in a college here in the States for several months, a professor noticed he spent all his spare time in the library. He saw he was a puzzled man looking for some answers to something, so he approached him with the question: "I notice you spend many hours here in the library, do you min-d telling me what you are searching for?" Here is his answer:

Holding out his New Testament he said:

"This book was given to me by a missionary from your country. He gave it to me and asked me to read it. As I read it I found out about a most wonderful person named Jesus Christ. This book says He is God's Son who came into this world to die for man's sins. He's the most wonderful person I ever heard of. He's good, kind, loving and just. After He died, and rose again, He went back to His Father in heaven, but He left followers called Apostles who are just like Him. They too are good, kind, loving, and just.

For several years I watched this missionary from your country who gave me this book. He is just like Jesus and His apostles. Then I accepted Jesus as my Saviour and Lord so that I too might be like Him.

Then as I talked to this missionary about where he got this book, he told me that in the United States nearly every home has one or several Bibles. In fact, he told me it was through people in churches back here giving of their money that made it possible for him to come to China. Then I told him of my desire to go to school in this country. He helped me make all the necessary arrangements. I just couldn't wait to get to a country where everybody is a Christian like my missionary friend.

Since I have been here I have talked to many people who say they are Christians, I have gone to a number of churches and have met many people who call themselves Christians, but I am very upset. My problem is this. My Jesus is so wonderful, He lived a wonderful life, His disciples were wonderful people just like Him, but Christians here today are just like my people in China who are not Christians. What I am doing is reading Church History to find out when Christians quit being like Jesus."

An illustration like this surely behooves us to open the Word of God regularly to see Jesus in all His beauty, all the time desiring the Holy Spirit to *"change us into the same image from glory unto glory."* This is a work of the Holy Spirit that should be a continuous experience with all God's children.

Chapter V

Spiritual Gifts - Tools or Toys, Which?

I CORINTHIANS 12:4 Now there are diversities of gifts, but the same Spirit.

I CORINTHIANS 14:1 Follow after charity, and desire spiritual gifts...

THESE verses are quoted from the passage of Scripture that has caused more interest (and also more confusion) among zealous professing Christians over the past two decades than all other Scriptures combined. I use the term "zealous professing Christians" because I am convinced that among those with this renewed spiritual interest there is a mixture of the genuine and the empty professors. In the last chapter we discussed the difference between "abiding fruit" and "passing experiences." I believe there are many of each of these two kinds of people among the great number who dwell on these three chapters: I CORINTHIANS 12, 13 and 14.

These three chapters are usually approached in one of two ways, depending with which camp one is identified. Both camps have preconceived ideas. The one will lay all the emphasis upon "experiencing the operation of the gifts mentioned" (especially tongues and healing), while the ether (through much exegesis) tries to prove the temporality of certain of these gifts. One camp seems to be saying,

"Our experiences prove our interpretations of these Scriptures" while the other says, "This is what these scriptures teach, forget experiences." A similar situation existed in the Church of England some two hundred years ago. The result was "The experience people" breaking away and starting the Methodist Church.

In this chapter we will take neither of the two approaches mentioned above. Instead we will first consider the purpose of spiritual gifts and then take a look at their method of use. Let us also mention here that there are other passages in God's Word that speak of gifts. We will make reference as we go along to some of these also.

A Practical Illustration

In the fourteenth chapter, where the apostle deals primarily with the use and misuse of one of these spiritual gifts (namely tongues), he uses a key word that will be used in our approach to an understanding of the purpose of all spiritual gifts. That word is "edify" in one of its forms. It appears in verses 3, 4, 5, 12, 17, 19, and 26. The word simply means "to build or construct." Therefore the purpose of spiritual gifts is to build or construct for the glory of God. This thought immediately eliminates many of the so-called manifestations of spiritual gifts. To many, spiritual gifts are toys to play with for personal enjoyment rather than tools to use in building for the glory of God. A personal illustration here might serve to make this clear.

My grandfather was a carpenter by trade. In the late 1800's and early 1900's he was known as one of the best in the part of the state of Pennsylvania in which he lived. Upon his death he left his tools to his son-in-law who was my father. My father knew nothing about building and therefore had a light esteem for my grandfather's tools. They were stored in two large chest-type tool boxes in our summer house. As my brother and I grew up we often admired these tools and asked many questions about them which Dad could not answer. Many hours were passed with great enjoyment as my brother and I "played" with these tools. Oh, we would never have admitted then that we were "playing" with them. We were "building" but we were building "playthings and playhouses" for our own fun and enjoyment

Over a period of years we lost many of grandfather's tools and ruined many others through misuse, such as cutting into nails and letting them lay out in the weather to rust and rot. My brother now has the tools that remain but they are in pretty bad shape because of our misuse of them.

A short time ago I was visiting my home area where our family has lived for generations. I searched in vain for any of the things my brother and I built with grandfather's tools. Nothing was to be found anywhere. But there stands grandfather's house which he built in 1889 with those tools along with a number of other structures he built long before I ever existed. What made the difference? Simply this, to grandfather those two chests contained "tools" to be used to build useful structures while to my brother and myself those chests contained "toys" to play with for our own enjoyment.

A Practical Admonition

It doesn't require a very careful examination to discover how many who claim to possess spiritual gifts see them and their purpose. "Tongues" or languages on the day of Pentecost (ACTS 2) was a tool in the ministry of the Apostles to begin the construction of the church. I would just like to ask a searching question here. How much of the present-day manifestation of the "gift of tongues" is used to construct and build lives for God's Glory? And lest I be misunderstood let me ask another question. How much of the building being done by those who believe "tongues have ceased" is of a permanent nature for the Glory of God? It would seem to me that all of us who claim to be co-laborers with God would be wise to do a little meditating on Paul's admonition in

I CORINTHIANS 3:10 . . . let every man take heed how he buildeth thereupon.

Paul was the wise masterbuilder whom God had chosen to lay the foundation for His church. I CORINTHIANS 3:9—11. Many through the centuries have built upon that foundation and we are still building upon it today. The big question each builder should be asking himself is, "What does my building consist of: that which abides, or that which will pass away? The answer to this question involves three things, only one of which we are discussing in this chapter. They are MATERIALS, METHODS, and MEANS (tools). The infallible Word of God surely gives clear instruction in each of these three areas. The problem is that only too often our zeal or ignorance is the governing factor in our building, instead of The Holy Spirit through His Inspired Word.

The great emphasis in our day is "personal happiness." The philosophy of the world is that happiness is the goal; anything that contributes toward that end is good. The "gifts of the Spirit" looked upon as toys and playthings fits in beautifully with this philosophy. As one studies the Word of God there is nothing to be found that would teach that happiness is not good. But one also discovers that most of God's choicest saints did not have very happy lives. Most carried heavy burdens and responsibilities and suffered persecutions that caused much more unhappiness than pleasure. Of course these saints walked by faith knowing that

> ROMANS 8:18...the sufferings of this present time are not worthy to be compared with the glory which shall be revealed in us.

"Future glory" meant far more to them than "present happiness." In other words, the inward satisfaction of knowing God was pleased with their lives now and a hope of sharing His Glory in eternity was far more important than present personal happiness. One cannot help but wonder what has happened to this philosophy among God's saints today.

Personal Happiness Philosophy

As one looks at Fundamental Christianity today, evidence of the "Personal Happiness Philosophy" abounds. The goal of salvation is personal happiness; the goal of a deeper spiritual life is personal happiness; the goal of discovering and exercising gifts is personal happiness. Appeal after appeal is "Come, get, receive to be happy." Is there any wonder so much unrest is to be found within the ranks of those who profess to know Jesus Christ in a personal way? As one man of God put it:

Most Christians today want a God to save them, keep them, give them His gifts, get them out of troubles, give them His blessings, and eventually take them to Heaven — but all this without allowing Him to govern them now.

That kind of a God does not exist. When the gospel of grace is preached in such a way that presents God as the giver, and man the receiver without repentance and. submission on man's part, grace becomes a disgrace. The result of such teaching neither glorifies God nor makes man happy.

When my son was four years old I was building an extra bedroom and a half bath on to the parsonage. I would work at it in my spare moments, an hour now and an hour then. Although it was winter and quite cold my son always wanted to be with me while I was working in these rooms. Time and again he would pick up one of the tools I was using for the project and want to "help". As much as I tried to explain to him that I was using those tools in a certain manner in order to "build," all he could see was what fun I was having as I "played" with those tools. He wanted in on the "fun" too. One day when I went to work on the rooms, I found he had decided to help Dad out. His tool was a hammer and his materials were nails. What fun he must have had pounding those nails into the new dry wall I had just finished installing several days before. Needless to say, my time that day was spent repairing the damage he had done using my tools as toys.

Although this chapter deals primarily with "gifts of the Spirit" let's take just a few moments and consider the greatest "Tool" God has given us to use in building lives for His Glory. That is His Word His Word is

JEREMIAH 23:29...like a hammer that breaketh the rock in pieces.

What a tremendous tool for a man of God with spiritual discernment to use to break a hardened sinful heart. Nathan, the prophet used it skillfully to break David's sin-hardened heart. But can you imagine what would have happened if Nathan would have kept pounding away at David's already broken heart? That's what my boy did with my hammer on a finished wall. I have no doubt but that I saw this done in the church in which I was reared many times. Once God's Word as a hammer has broken the stony heart that one needs "the Balm of Gilead," not more pounding. This illustrates another aspect concerning the use of God's gifts as well as His Word. That is the need of skill.

Learning To Use The Tools

Once I do get to the place of maturity where 1 understand that God's gifts are tools not toys and I do recognize that the important thing is not using God's gifts far personal enjoyment but to build for His Glory, I must begin to learn skills. That is, I must learn to rightly use whatever God has given me. In reality I must learn to live in the Spirit so that He may do His Work first in, and then, through me. In dealing with another life I must know when, where and how to use whatever God has given me in order to bring that one into a right relationship and fellowship with God. Or to use the analogy of a building I must understand how to use God's tools He has given me to build people into living stones in His Temple. (I PETER 2:5 and EPHESIANS 2:19—22)

During the past fifteen years I have heard so much controversy over which tools (gifts) are available today that I wonder if this is not a major trick of Satan to make us skeptical and fearful anytime we hear the term "gifts of the Spirit." Forgetting for a moment the skillful use of the Spirit's gifts I wonder how many of God's children are even aware if they possess any of His gifts. It is my observation that most of us have been so busy proving our position on what we call "sign" gifts that we have completely passed over our tremendous need for any of the gifts. Instead of humbly waiting upon The Holy Spirit to enlighten us with an open Bible before us, we begin quoting all the "authorities" we have read on the subject. How can The Holy Spirit ever reveal to any Christian a gift he might possess and enable him to become skillful in its use if all our time is spent reading and studying other "authorities" instead of the Word of God?

We also face another great obstacle in this area. In this day of "modern Gnosticism" the church as a whole has allowed itself to accept the world's philosophy of education. That is, that the only truly educated person is the one who has spent untold hours in the classrooms of higher education. Most Christians put far more confidence in the statements of highly academically educated men than the man who has gotten his education some other way. Although this may be valid reasoning in many areas, it certainly is not when it comes to Biblical spiritual matters. According to the Word of God the first and most important qualification to gaining knowledge and wisdom is a *"fear [reverential trust in] of the Lord"* PROVERBS 1:7. In the second place is a hunger so strong for truth that one will put forth every possible effort in his search of the Scriptures, even to the point of crying to God for knowledge and understanding. PROVERBS 2:1—5. And lastly, a recognition that spiritual things are *"spiritually discerned"*. I CORINTHIANS 2:9—16. It's not a matter of how intelligent, how educated (academically) or what do the "authorities" say, but rather, am I a spiritual man thinking with the mind of Christ? Combining the titles of four hymns let's all ask ourselves this question:

How Long Has It Been (Since I spent a)...
Sweet Hour of Prayer...
Sitting at The Feet of Jesus (asking Him to)...
Speak to Me That I Might Speak(?)

The Child of God who practices this with an open Bible soon becomes an authority on spiritual matters. This is all said, not as a knock against academic education, but rather to hopefully get

God's children to see that academic education is no substitute for the teaching ministry of the Holy Spirit.

This "modern day gnosticism" has caused two sad results in the church today. First it has caused the average Christian to feel that knowledge, gifts and skills required in God's Work are best, when learned, or in some people's minds, only learned in academic classrooms. This kind of thinking leads to the second one which is the idea that most of God's Work must be done by academically trained professionals. According to the Apostle Paul's letter to the Corinthian Church, each member in the body of Christ has a ministry and is necessary to the edifying of the entire body.

If you are in the Body of Christ do you know of any "spiritual gifts" you possess? If you do, is it to you a toy to play with for your own benefit and happiness or is it a tool to build with for the Glory of God?

Chapter VI

Filled With The Spirit or Just Excited — Which?

EPHESIANS 5:18 Be not drunk with wine, wherein is excess; but be filled with the Spirit.

THE EXPRESSIONS "full of The Holy Spirit" and "filled with The Spirit" occur a number of times throughout the New Testament. On the day of Pentecost the Disciples

ACTS 2:4...were all filled with The Holy Spirit and began to speak with other tongues, as The Spirit gave them utterance.

A short time later the same group of people (although increased somewhat in number) were again filled with The Holy Spirit. ACTS 4:31. At the first persecution of the early Church the Apostle Peter is said to have been filled with The Holy Spirit as he answered the council before whom he had been brought. ACTS 4:8. When this early Church recognized the need for deacons (servants) to take care of the temporal matters that were essential to their Christian testimony, they sought out

ACTS 6:3 . . . men of honest report full of The Holy Spirit and wisdom to appoint over these business matters.

From these and other Scriptures which speak of the *"filling of The Spirit"* we become aware of the absolute necessity of this experience to empower and enable God's people to do His work and maintain a testimony honoring to Him.

In this chapter let us look at three aspects of the Bible's teaching on this subject. First, the Biblical teaching on God's method of filling His people with His Spirit; secondly, His purpose for filling His people with Himself; and last the evidence of "The filling of The Holy Spirit."

The first thing that we must be abundantly clear on in our thinking is that every child of God is indwelt by The Holy Spirit. The Apostle Paul tells us,

ROMANS 8:9... if any man have not The Spirit of Christ he is none of His.

When he wrote to the bickering, carnal, Christians at Corinth he even told them (and very emphatically) that they were the temples of The Holy Spirit. I CORINTHIANS 3:16 and 6:19—20. The teaching that a person can become a child of God through the New Birth and sometime later receive The Holy Spirit is foreign to the Word of God. In fact, the key passage on the New Birth (JOHN 3) teaches that the New Birth is performed by The Holy Spirit imparting life to the human spirit. The word "life" itself means "union." When the New Birth occurs, there is an eternal union of God's Spirit and man's spirit and that one in whom this takes place is spiritually alive. Therefore, the filling of The Spirit can in no way be described as The Spirit coming in to dwell and certainly cannot be a returning to indwell once again one in whom He has already performed the New Birth. Christ promised His disciples that when The Comforter (The Holy Spirit) would come He would abide with them forever. JOHN 14:16.

Now then, let us take a look at God's method of filling with His Spirit. Two incidents in the Gospel of John and the passage in EPHESIANS quoted at the beginning of this chapter, make clear what God meant when He said to be filled with The Spirit. In John, chapter four, our Lord, while passing through Samaria met a Samaritan woman at Jacob's well. After a short conversation concerning the well and literal water He said to her

JOHN 4:13 . . . Whosoever drinketh of this water shall thirst again:

14 But whosoever drinketh of the water that I shall give him shall never thirst; but the water that I shall give him shall be in him a well of water springing up into everlasting life.

The picture here is that of an artesian well, that is, a well that is constantly overflowing. How fortunate is the home with an artesian well, where no pump or buckets are needed to get the water out of that hole in the ground; and how blessed is that Christian who recognizes he is an artesian well from whom the Living Water (The Holy Spirit) is to continuously flow without a lot of regular priming, pumping, or dipping.

Again in JOHN 7 we read of an incident that took place in the Temple. Here our Lord is explaining to the people present some of the truths concerning His Messianic ministry. He closes his teaching there with these words:

JOHN 7:37 . . If any man thirst, let him come unto me, and drink.

38 He that believeth on me, as the Scripture hath said, out of his belly [innermost being] shall flow rivers of living water.

And then John explains what Christ meant by these words. He says:

JOHN 7:39 (But this spake He of The Spirit which they that believe on Him should receive: for The Holy Ghost was not yet given; because that Jesus was not yet glorified.)

The picture again is clear. It is that of a fountain flowing forth continuously, producing streams of water. And again I say, Blessed is that Christian who sees himself a fountain from whom The Living Water (The Holy Spirit) continually flows. For that one there is no more straining and struggling to get a little of that Living Water to come forth. The same teaching is to be found in JOHN 15 in the picture of the vine and branches. The branches simply abide in the vine and bear the fruit the life from the vine produces.

How clear these pictures all became many years ago as I was studying EPHESIANS 5:18. There is the command to be filled with The Spirit. As I was studying I noticed the verb was a continuous action verb. Translated literally the command would be *"Be ye being filled with The Spirit."* The command is the same as the pictures in JOHN'S gospel. As the well is an overflowing well from an ever-lasting source and the fountain comes from an endless supply so there is to be a continuous overflowing resulting from a continuous filling. How different from so much of the teaching that pictures the Christian as a cistern that in one way or another gets filled, uses up the energy from that filling, and then returns to be filled again.

Another illustration used in this modem age pictures the Christian as running on batteries. He often speaks of having to get his batteries recharged. The idea is that like an electric piece of equipment running on batteries which are not constantly being charged as the equipment is being used (therefore regularly in need of recharging), so the Christian must regularly or at least occasion-ally get recharged (revived). A pastor once told me the church of which he was pastor would die were it not for the annual revival where the people could have their batteries recharged. For those who live in this manner with their lives a series of "ups and downs" determined by the amount of charge in their batteries, I ask the ques-tion which is the title of this chapter "FILLED WITH THE SPIRIT OR JUST EXCITED — WHICH?"

There is nothing wrong with excitement, enthusiasm, and zeal if it is generated by the indwelling Holy Spirit, but excitement, enthu-siasm and zeal that needs to be primed, pushed and persuaded to be kept going are surely not from the indwelling Spirit. Then too, when one sees these qualities easily replaced by indifference and uncon-cern, how can anyone claim them to be a work of God's Spirit? No, the Biblical description of The Filling of The Spirit is that of a continuous flowing from an endless source producing the kind of energy that is needed to fulfill the command of

I CORINTHIANS 15:58 Therefore, my beloved brethren, be ye steadfast, unmovable, ALWAYS abounding in the work of the Lord...

This brings us to our next point, THE PURPOSE FOR THE FILLING OF THE SPIRIT. As one listens to many of the testimonies given by religious people today, you would be led to believe *"The fitting of The Spirit"* was solely to make one feel good. The whole philosophy of the world today has as its goal "emotionally happiness." And in striving to reach this goal there has been produced more "emotional unhappiness" than ever before. It's sad to say, but it's true that much religious teaching of today has the same philosophy. It goes something like this: Accept Christ and be happy, Be Born Again and be happy, Be baptized in The Spirit and be happy, Be filled with The Spirit and be happy. Now happiness is a good emotional feeling that is a result of pleasant happenings, surroundings, and circumstances, and all of us should be thankful to God that He allows many of these to come our way.

But the purpose God has in granting Spiritual experiences is NOT our emotional happiness. And especially, the filling of His Spirit is NOT primarily for our emotional welfare, but rather (as we said of His Gifts in the last chapter) that we might be to the praise of His glory and accomplish the work He has for us to do. On the Day of Pentecost He filled the disciples in order that they might make Him known to all the different peoples who were visiting Jerusalem on those feast days. The first Deacons were to be men full of The Holy Spirit that they might serve Him well in temporal matters. Paul was to be filled with The Holy Spirit in order to proclaim the Word of God in Power to the Gentiles. The Christians in ACTS were filled with The Holy Spirit so they could speak the Word of God with boldness. Today we are to be filled with The Holy Spirit for the same reasons as well as to meet the many new challenges and temptations we face that those in the first century did not. There is absolutely no way we can accomplish our supreme reason for being, apart from a continuous filling and overflowing of His indwelling Spirit. Let us also make sure that we understand the command to be filled with The Spirit is a command to all believers, not just to those in what we so often call "fulltime Christian Service." Every Christian needs the constant filling if he or she is going to be constantly overflowing. This constant overflowing is what makes our Christian Testimony attractive to the lost and glorifying to God.

This brings us to our third point which is "THE EVIDENCE OF BEING FILLED WITH THE SPIRIT."

Many years ago during a conversation with a person from a certain group which speaks much of The Holy Spirit I was told that I did not believe in "the evidence of The Spirit." Upon questioning what was meant by that statement I was told that "speaking in unknown tongues" was the evidence of The Spirit, and until I had that experience I could not claim the baptism or filling of the Spirit (This person made no distinction between the baptism and filling.) As always I asked for Biblical support for this teaching. The only support given was from ACTS 2 where the disciples

ACTS 2:4. . . spake with other tongues, as The Spirit gave them utterance.

The fact that many other passages of Scripture taught other evidences of The Spirit's filling meant nothing to this individual. It is one of these passages that we shall look at now.

The verse quoted from EPHESIANS 5 at the beginning of this chapter gives the command to be filled with The Spirit and the following verses give the evidences that will result in the life of one who is filled with the Spirit. Keep in mind that the filling with the Spirit is a continuous process, therefore, the evidences are to be continuous evidences.

EPHESIANS 5:19 tells us that the inward life of one filled with The Spirit will be one of continual praise to God. In the words of Scripture the one filled with The Spirit will be "Speaking to himself in psalms and hymns and spiritual songs, singing and making melody in his heart to the Lord." A hymn writer many years ago put it this way.

"This is my story, this is my song,
Praising my Saviour all the day long."

In many quarters today the idea is that it is more important to have a time-place experience than to have a continuous experience within of praise flowing to God. Who can say how many there are in this category who speak of a past experience of being filled with The Spirit while their present inward life is empty as far as praise toward God is concerned. If only each one of us would be honest enough to give ourself an objective evaluation as to our own inner life. Certainly no one else can do that for us. The only ones who know for sure what our inner life is like are God and ourselves. How foolish I would be to claim to be filled with God's Spirit when instead of praise filling my inner being there is emptiness, or, even worse, murmuring, complaining and criticism. Instead of a continuous "melody in our hearts to the Lord" I am afraid He often hears a conglomeration of noises in the midst of which are heard only occasionally some melodious sounds.

The second evidence mentioned in EPHESIANS 5:20 is a thankful heart or again to put it in the exact words of Scripture

EPHESIANS 5:20 Giving thanks always for all things unto God and the Father in the name of our Lord Jesus Christ.

This evidence is an evidence of attitude. Attitudes are seen of people as well as of God. Notice again the word *"always"* — Speaking of a continuous thankful attitude. Again we must say, how foolish it is to claim to be filled with The Spirit while our attitude manifests far more complaining about things that are wrong, or things we don't have, rather than an attitude of thanksgiving for the undeserved blessings we have received from a loving Heavenly Father. Andrew Murray said late in the last century that the greatest sin of God's people was "ingratitude." And things have certainly not improved over the past hundred years. Only a Biblical understanding of "Grace" and a continuous filling of The Indwelling Spirit can bring about a permanent attitude of Thanksgiving, When this is evident in a life you can be sure that Christian is experiencing a filling of the Holy Spirit.

The third evidence that will be manifested in one filled with the Holy Spirit is in verse 21. It is a "Submissive Spirit," or again to quote Scripture verbatim,

EPHESIANS 5:21 Submitting yourselves one to another in the fear of God.

If you want to see this kind of a submissive spirit portrayed read and re-read the Gospels. Jesus Christ lived a submissive life continually. He never, as a man, insisted on His rights. He submitted Himself to the misunderstandings of all (family, friends and enemies alike) eventually to submit to false accusers and unjust condemnation of all sorts without retaliation of any kind. This He did not as God (which He surely always was) but as a Man who was always filled with The Spirit without measure. (JOHN 3:34).

Let us just look at one aspect of this submissive spirit that is an evidence of one who is filled with The Spirit. That is, that this submission is not only toward God but *"one to another."* It is one thing to submit to God who has every right to our yieldedness and quite another to submit to others who may be constantly insisting on their own rights. It is natural to want our own way. This spirit is manifest in each of us from the earliest years of our childhood. It is supernatural to submit to the desires of others. Only one filled with The Spirit will live a constant life of submission not only to God but to others. Let us just make sure we are only speaking of those areas where there is no sin involved. No one who is filled with The Spirit will ever submit to another's ways or will if to do so would involve one in some sinful act or practice.

In closing, may each of us be willing to put the test spoken of in these verses to ourselves. Do *I* have the evidences of the filling of The Spirit spoken of here? There are, first, an inward life of singing, praise and making melody to God; secondly, manifesting a thankful attitude; and thirdly, living a submissive life toward one another. There are certainly many other evidences of the Spirit's presence and filling, but where these three are not present in a life it would be foolish to claim any experiences as an expression of God's Indwelling Spirit.

After looking at what our Lord taught about the filling of the Spirit and looking here in EPHESIANS 5, and then comparing these teachings with many present-day teachings and experiences, do you see why we would ask the question, "FILLED WITH THE SPIRIT OR JUST EXCITED — WHICH?"

CPSIA information can be obtained at www.ICGtesting.com
Printed in the USA
LVOW130607080213

319158LV00001B/136/P